Good Housekeeping Home Handbook

Good Housekeeping

Home Handbook

The ultimate survival guide to
running your home

Edited by Linda Zeff

COLLINS & BROWN

First published in Great Britain in 2003 by
Collins & Brown Limited
64 Brewery Road
London N7 9NT

A member of **Chrysalis** Books plc

Published in association with The National
Magazine Company Limited

Good Housekeeping is a registered trademark
of The National Magazine Company Limited

9 8 7 6 5 4 3 2 1

British Library Cataloguing-in-Publication
Data: A catalogue record for this book is
available from the British Library

ISBN: 185585 998 X

Designed by Roger Hammond
Project managed by Emma Baxter
Copy-edited by Jude Ledger

Colour reproduction by Tennon & Polert
Colour
Scanning, Hong Kong
Printed by Imago Singapore

CONTENTS

HOW THIS HANDBOOK WORKS

THE GOOD HOUSEKEEPING HOME HANDBOOK gives the solutions to hundreds of commonly asked household queries in one easy-to-use guide. It is divided into three main parts – **Buying**, **Care and cleaning** and **Problem solving** – plus a **Directory**. Each part consists of four or five chapters packed with tried and tested advice, listed alphabetically. As well as the index and the part and chapter contents, we have provided a wealth of fact boxes, tips and cross-references to lead you to the piece of information you need as swiftly as possible.

Part 1, **BUYING**, will help you shop with confidence. Every year the Good Housekeeping Institute tests hundreds of household appliances and other products, and carries out research on dozens of services. For this handbook, we have distilled that experience and expertise into reliable advice that you can use when you need to re-equip your kitchen, replace your carpet or find a reliable tradesman.

Part 2, **CARE AND CLEANING**, is designed to help you keep everything in your home in good condition. Once again, the Good Housekeeping Institute's painstaking tests come into their own, allowing us to tell you which proprietary products – and which low-cost household remedies – will really get rid of stains, marks and general grubbiness on your furniture, clothes and other goods.

Part 3, **PROBLEM SOLVING**, gives advice when you need it most. As well as a straightforward first aid guide, it includes guidance on pest control and simple repairs, and on how to complain effectively about goods and services.

Part 4, the **DIRECTORY**, is the Good Housekeeping Institute's own invaluable contacts book, listing all the products, suppliers and useful organisations mentioned in the Home Handbook.

We have made every effort to check that all the information in the book is as comprehensive, accurate and up-to-date as possible, but if you have any comments, queries or tips for the next edition of Home Handbook, please E-mail them at GHhomehandbook@natmags.co.uk.

Good Housekeeping

Within two years of its launch in 1922, *Good Housekeeping* magazine set up its own Institute to test products, provide advice and champion the rights of consumers. As well as producing test reports and many other practical features in the magazine, the Good Housekeeping Institute responds to more than 5,000 requests a year for information and advice.

Advice lines
This is a premium-rate live service.
Lines are open Fridays only (11am–5pm)
Product/household advice Tel: 0906 752 9070
Food and cookery Tel: 0906 752 9080

Write for advice:
Ask the Good Housekeeping Institute,
72 Broadwick Street,
London W1F 9EP
E-mail for advice:
consumer.query@natmags.co.uk **or** cookery.query@natmags.co.uk

PART 1

Buying

AROUND 60 PER CENT of the enquiries received by the Good Housekeeping Institute every year concern products – which ones to choose and where to find them. Whether you are buying new or replacing old goods, Part 1 contains a wealth of practical information – from how to understand the 'jargon' found on sales literature to how to decide which features are worth paying extra for.

You will also find advice about your consumer rights, shopping from home, and when it pays to shop around – for everything from appliances to services.

THE 'GHI APPROVED' LOGO
The GHI Approved logo can be found on a range of kitchen appliances and other products that meet the Institute's quality standards. For more information, visit www.goodhousekeeping.co.uk/ghi.html or write to Good Housekeeping Institute (Accreditation), 72 Broadwick Street, London W1F 9EP.

Safe shopping

IN THIS CHAPTER YOU WILL FIND

Whether you are buying goods, paying for a service or shopping on the internet, these guidelines will help you shop safely and well.

Know your rights

SEE ALSO

Complaining, p.247

WHEN YOU BUY GOODS

Goods must be of satisfactory quality (durable, safe and free from minor defects), fit for their purpose (including any purpose mentioned by you that the retailer has agreed to) and exactly as described.

WHEN YOU PAY FOR A SERVICE

Any service, for example, from a hairdresser, builder or car repairer, should be carried out with reasonable skill and care, within a reasonable time and at a reasonable charge if no price has been fixed in advance.

WHEN YOU BUY BY CREDIT CARD

Using your credit card gives you added protection for items over £100 in value. If you have a problem and complaining to the retailer has got you nowhere (or the retailer has gone out of business), you will be able to claim against the card issuer. Some card issuers say they do not honour transactions made abroad, but you do not have to accept this policy.

►

5 THINGS TO KNOW IF YOU ARE UNHAPPY WITH GOODS OR SERVICES

1. You are within your rights to **cancel goods and services** if they have not been delivered, or work has not been completed by an agreed date.
2. The **responsibility for faulty goods** lies with the retailer, not the manufacturer.
3. You have the **same rights when you buy in a sale** as at any other time – goods should be free of defects, apart from any specifically pointed out to you when you buy.
4. There is **no set time limit** on returning faulty goods – you do not automatically lose your rights after a certain period, but it is wise to return them or inform the retailer as soon as you notice the problem (see If things go wrong, p.246).
5. Firms **cannot disclaim responsibility** for loss or damage to your property just by putting up a sign saying they do.

Shopping from home

SEE ALSO

If things go wrong, p.246

If you shop from home – whether by phone, mail order or the internet – there are new regulations that give you extra rights on top of those set out above. However, these rights do not apply to videos, computer software or travel or event tickets. You are entitled to:

- Clear information before placing an order (such as the trader's contact details and policy on returning/exchanging goods).
- Written confirmation (by letter, fax or E-mail) of purchases.
- A 'cooling-off' period during which you can cancel the order and get a refund.
- A full refund if the goods do not arrive on time (within 30 days or on an agreed date).
- Protection if anyone uses your credit or debit card fraudulently.

TIP

For a free advice leaflet on shopping from home, contact the Office of Fair Trading.

INTERNET SHOPPING

Before buying goods via the internet, make sure you are dealing with a reputable company. The following details should be included on the retailer's website:

- The full name and postal address of the company – not just its E-mail address – and its phone number, so you know who you are dealing with and how to get in touch if things go wrong.
- How long it will take for the items to be delivered.
- The company's refund policy.
- A reminder of your cancellation rights. You can change your mind and send items back within seven days of receiving them, although some goods such as food and travel tickets are not covered.
- What data the company is collecting about you, how it will be used and for how long it will be stored.

INTERNET SECURITY

Make sure your credit card details do not fall into the wrong hands when you shop online.

- In a credit card transaction, you are sharing valuable information. Only do it if you trust the company you are buying from.
- Never type in your details on a site that does not promise security or encryption facilities. Look for the closed padlock or unbroken key symbol in the corner of the 'page' or check that the page address starts https:// and not just http://.

Opt for sites with the TrustUK logo. These sites must collect and hold your credit card details securely, and keep them only as long as is necessary for the transaction. For more details and links to 'E-hallmarked' sites, visit the TrustUK website.

When it pays to shop around

Here's how to find the best deals on appliances, utilities and household services – and how to avoid rip-offs and false economies.

Appliances

SEE ALSO

10 ways to secure a bargain, p.16

When it comes to appliances the best savings are usually to be found on the internet – but it always pays to shop around. Remember, though, that delivery costs could wipe out part or all of the apparent advantage, and prices do not remain static – internet retailers, in particular, may alter prices from one day to the next, so grab good deals when you can.

PRICE-MATCHING PLEDGES

Many stores offer price-matching or price-beating pledges – under these schemes, if you find the identical product in a competitor's outlet for a lower price after you have bought it, the store will refund the difference or even beat the lower price. In most cases, you can also use a competitor's lower price to claim a discount before you buy. Pledges usually cover only local shops and have a time limit for claiming.

Extended warranties

Extended warranties provide cover for the cost of repairs on an electrical appliance, usually lasting for three to five years – overlapping with the manufacturer's one-year guarantee. Many offer extra benefits beyond simple breakdown insurance, such as accidental damage, theft or new-for-old replacement cover. But before you sign up, check exactly what ▶

10 WAYS TO SECURE A BARGAIN

1. Start with the **name and full model number** of the product you want, so you can easily check the price in your favourite shop over the phone or through its website, if it has one.
2. Be **ready to switch** to an all-but-identical model, or one lacking a feature you don't need.
3. Look for **special offers** on discontinued or superseded models that retailers want to clear.
4. If you're not fussy about what model you want and you belong to a **discount warehouse club** – or can shop with someone who does – you may be able to pick up a bargain.
5. **Shop around** at a few outlets, including at least one with a price-matching promise.
6. If you are happy to buy over the internet, start by **trawling for the best bargains** using a site such as www.pricerunner.com, which checks the prices of both high-street and online retailers. But don't assume the internet will always beat the high street for the specific model you want, once all charges are taken into account.
7. Don't assume nationwide chains will always beat a **local independent retailer** on price.
8. Check whether **delivery, fitting** and any other charges are included in the price – if not, don't forget to ask how much they are and add them on before making comparisons. Check whether delivery arrangements suit you and whether the retailer will get rid of your old appliance, and take into account the peace-of-mind value of dealing with an easily contacted firm you know and trust.
9. Ask if any **add-ons** are included, such as a free extra year's warranty.
10. Try doing a deal – you may be able to **negotiate a discount** for buying two or more items, or have delivery, fitting or a warranty thrown in.

the warranty is giving you that you don't already have through the manufacturer's free guarantee. Having trusted, reliable tradesmen in your address book will put you in a stronger position when weighing up whether or not to opt for a warranty.

Extended warranties

GETTING THE BEST DEAL

Warranties earn good commission for sales staff who will try hard to sell you the retailer's warranty, but do not feel pressured. Ask how long you have to decide if you want the policy – it's usually 14 days after you have bought the item, which gives you time to check out other options. There is usually a 14-28 day cancellation period, too, so all is not lost if you buy a retailer's warranty then find a better deal elsewhere. These are your main options:

- **The manufacturer:** if you remember to send off the guarantee card for your appliance, you will receive details of the manufacturer's warranty scheme that will provide cover for the first year. But don't wait – ring for details, or it may be too late to cancel a retailer's policy if you opted for one.
- **Insurance companies:** domestic & General offers accidental damage and breakdown cover for any brand of appliance less than eight years old. Both Domestic & General and Norwich Union Direct offer multi-appliance policies – if you have several appliances, these are much more cost-effective than taking out numerous individual warranties.
- **Utility companies:** kitchen Appliance Care from British Gas can cover appliances of any age.

WHERE THE WARRANTY COMES FREE

- If you buy a large electrical appliance (from washing machines to hi-fis) at John Lewis, you will be given a year's free warranty in addition to the manufacturer's guarantee.
- Asda offers its customers a free three-year warranty on 'anything with a plug' that you buy in the store. This runs alongside the manufacturer's standard guarantee.
- If you use certain credit cards to buy electrical goods, your new appliances will be covered by a free warranty when you register them with the card provider. The warranty usually ▶

gives one to two years' extra breakdown cover after the manufacturer's guarantee has expired. Cards offering this service include Barclaycard (Classic and Gold), Lloyds TSB Asset Advance and Natwest Gold.

COMPARING COSTS

If you are set on buying a warranty, compare the policies and decide which specific benefits you need. Check that you are not duplicating cover you have elsewhere (such as home contents or travel insurance). Better policies provide a brand new appliance if yours cannot be fixed during the warranty period.

- Comet will also transfer the remaining cover on your warranty to the new appliance.
- Dixons/Currys prides itself on its speedy response times.
- Hotpoint says it uses only its own engineers and genuine Hotpoint parts.
- John Lewis's TV cover is free because it is basic breakdown cover and does not include any frills such as accidental damage.

Fuel suppliers

To find out if switching gas and/or electricity supplier would save you money, there are a number of organisations that can do the calculations for you, based on where you live and your usage of power. These are listed on the website of Energywatch, the gas and electricity consumer watchdog, and include uSwitch (www.uswitch.com, Tel: 0845 601 2856), www.buy.co.uk, www.ukpower.co.uk, www.unravelit.com, and www.saveonyourbills.co.uk. Many of these organisations also do a similar job on your phone deal and other services.

5 THINGS YOU SHOULD KNOW ABOUT CHANGING FUEL SUPPLIERS

1. Collect a **year's worth of bills** (make sure you're looking at actual usage based on meter readings, not just estimates).
2. **Don't expect big savings** if your bills are already small.
3. Many impressive-seeming savings may simply be down to switching to a **direct debit** deal, which would be cheaper if you stayed with your existing supplier.
4. Don't assume a **dual-fuel** deal will automatically save more.
5. If you're not happy with **sales tactics** used or the changeover doesn't go smoothly, contact the consumer watchdog Energywatch.

Telephone deals

If you want to save money on your telephone bills, there are a number of ways to do so. Here are your options:

Indirect access services If you're a BT customer, you can make cheaper calls by using different telephone companies. You access their service either by dialling a short code (or freephone number) before the normal phone number, or by plugging an autodialler box in between your socket and phone. Indirect access suppliers usually advertise in local papers or via mailshots, so look out for deals in your area.

Carrier pre-selection (CPS) If you do not want the hassle of having to dial extra numbers or getting an adapter, you can now 'pre-select' an alternative supplier for all or some types of call (eg calls to national numbers, mobiles, etc). These calls are then automatically routed via your chosen supplier. Telecoms regulator Oftel has a list of CPS operators on its website, www.oftel.gov.uk/publications/carrier/index.htm.

All-inclusive packages If your phone line is part of an all-inclusive TV and phone package from a cable company,

▶

your options for making cheaper calls may be more limited. You will not be able to use CPS, but a few indirect access operators, such as Tiscali and One.Tel, for example, offer their services to cable users.

WEBSITES WORTH A VISIT

There are a handful of websites that compare the tariffs of leading suppliers. For the names of services accredited by Oftel, visit www.oftel.gov.uk.

www.uSwitch.com Uses your postcode, existing supplier details and number/type of calls you make to help you work out the cheapest deal from 19 top suppliers, including how to optimise the deal with your existing supplier. uSwitch takes into account discounts, service and charging methods.

www.callforless.co.uk Makes general recommendations about the best suppliers for different types of call. It also has a useful comparison chart to help you identify which are the cheapest rates for worldwide destinations.

www.phonebills.org The only official Oftel-endorsed site, but with just four suppliers to compare, its use is limited.

HOW TO SHOP FOR THE BEST TELEPHONE DEAL

1. Identify the destinations, time and type of calls you make most often. The **biggest savings are on international calls**.
2. Compare like with like – BT's rivals tend to use the BT standard daytime rate to highlight maximum savings, so **ask for a direct comparison** with your existing discounts and ask questions: is there a minimum call charge or connection fee; do they bill by the second or minute; and does the package include any free minutes?
3. **Get the balance right** – low rates are no good if you cannot get through or if the line is so poor you cannot hear properly.

Tradesmen

If you need someone reliable and trustworthy to decorate your home, revamp your kitchen or plumb in a dishwasher, here are some helpful guidelines.

SEE ALSO

5 tips on buying a
new kitchen, p.58

OBTAINING RECOMMENDATIONS

If no-one you know can recommend someone, there are several ways to arrive at a shortlist of firms to ask for a quote:
- Through one of the find-a-tradesman schemes or trade associations.
- Via a local amenity or consumer group's list (your local council should be able to tell you how to contact these organisations; some councils even run their own 'reputable trader' lists).
- From your household insurer.
- Through your managing agent (if you live in a flat).
- By asking your neighbours and looking for signboards outside houses in your area.
- By looking in local newspapers and classified directories.

SEE ALSO

Trade Assocations,
p.23

TRADE ASSOCIATIONS AND LOGOS

Although many trade associations have codes of practice, the best of which include complaint handling and dispute resolution schemes run by an independent body, others have little to offer the customer. Here's how to check up on the logos.
- Contact the trade association to make sure the firm you plan to use is a current member.
- Ask how firms qualify – do they have to agree to a code of practice, for example, or provide evidence of good financial standing and workmanship?
- Find out how the association could help if you were

▶

dissatisfied with one of its members, and whether it has a dispute resolution scheme.

■ Ask what the association would be able to do if a member went bust or disappeared before your job was completed satisfactorily.

SHOPPING AROUND FOR QUALITY

Ask at least three firms for a quote and make it clear that you want to inspect at least one similar job before you give the go-ahead. Even with a relatively straightforward project, write down exactly what you want done before the tradesmen visit, so you can be certain you are comparing like with like.

WEBSITES WORTH A VISIT

The sites listed on pages 24 and 25 will help you track down individuals and firms in a wide range of specific trades willing to work in your area – although you should be aware that some cover only two or three areas.

5 WAYS TO AVOID THE COWBOYS

1. Don't even consider having a job done by someone 'doing work in your area' unless you can talk to at least one householder prepared to recommend their workmanship, reliability and punctuality.
2. Don't be swayed by time-limited 'special prices' – they could be specially high for that kind of work, so shop around.
3. By all means collect flyers put through your door, but check the tradesmen out thoroughly before you employ them.
4. Be wary of tradesmen you can only contact by phone, especially a mobile – if things go wrong, they are hard to find.
5. Don't suffer in silence – if you do get caught out, tell the trading standards department at your local council – your case could help stop someone else's home or bank balance being ruined.

TRADE ASSOCIATIONS

Contact details for all these trade associations are listed in the directory on page 265–275.

Electrical Contractors' Association
This association has a register of 2,000 'qualified and accountable' members who must follow a code of fair trading. All electrical work is covered by an insurance-backed warranty and bond scheme. The Electrical Contractors' Association of Scotland works in a similar way.

Federation of Master Builders
This federation has a code of practice, an arbitration scheme and an optional insurance-backed warranty scheme called MasterBond.

Heating and Ventilating Contractors' Association
This association has a consumer Code of Fair Trading that provides a complaints procedure including a conciliation service and referral to binding arbitration. It also includes a Guaranteed Installer scheme.

The Institute of Plumbing
There are 3,500 qualified and experienced members of this institute. Contact the institute for plumbers in your area.

National Federation of Roofing Contractors
Has a code of practice and optional one-year guarantee scheme.

CONSUMER PROTECTION BODIES

The Council for Registered Gas Installers (CORGI)
National watchdog for gas safety. UK gas fitters must register with CORGI by law. Ask to see a current ID photocard showing types of work the fitter is 'competent and qualified' to do. CORGI will take up safety complaints about any gas fitter.

National Inspection Council for Electrical Installation Contracting (NICEIC)
An independent consumer protection and electrical safety organisation. Maintains a roll of 10,000 approved contractors throughout the UK. Each contractor is annually assessed and is required to issue a signed certificate on completion of work, showing compliance with relevant safety standards.

▶

www.homepro.com (Homepro) Independent service that charges tradesmen a fee when it gives them work. Quick and easy to use, but limited coverage in some parts of the country. Offers insurance-backed guarantee for up to 10 years.

www.improveline.com (Improveline) Good site, with 150,000 contractors. All firms offer a minimum two-year guarantee on work carried out. For big projects, you type in details which Improveline pass to up to three tradesmen; if any are interested, it is then up to you to contact them. For smaller jobs, you just browse among local tradesmen.

www.qualityguild.co.uk (Quality Guild) Set up by Cumbria Training and Enterprise Council, Quality Guild covers Cumbria, South West Scotland, the Borders, Lancashire and the North East. Firms are thoroughly checked out, and must follow a code of conduct. If customer complaints are not resolved within a month, QG will step in.

10 THINGS TO WATCH OUT FOR WHEN AN ESTIMATE ARRIVES

1. Did it take **more than a week** to arrive? If so, be wary.
2. Is it written on **company letterhead**? Tatty bits of paper are not a good sign.
3. Does it include a **detailed breakdown** of costs and VAT?
4. Does it include **technical terms** or anything else you do not understand?
5. Does it indicate **how long** the job will take?
6. Do **quantities of raw materials** such as paint or timber vary between estimates? (Skimping on coats of paint may indicate that standards are not high enough, for example.)
7. Is it clear which, if any, materials are **included in the price**?
8. Will the firm agree a **fixed price contract** before starting, rather than just an estimate?
9. Is it clear when deposits and stage **payments** are expected?
10. Is the tradesman easy to get hold of, and happy to **answer your questions**?

10 IMPORTANT CONTRACT TIPS

1. Ask your local authority if you need **planning permission** or building regulations approval before you give the go-ahead for the work to be done.

2. Insist on a **written contract**, but think carefully about what you want done before you sign it. Changing your mind or asking for extras gives the firm a golden opportunity to inflate the bill.

3. Make sure the work specifies a **start date, completion date**, costs and cancellation rights.

4. Check if subcontractors are to be used, and **who is responsible** for the quality and timing of their work.

5. Make it part of the contract that an **agreed sum** is not to be exceeded without your written permission.

6. If the job is large, it is reasonable to agree to stage payments, but be suspicious of any company that asks for a sizeable deposit or money for materials; it may not have the funds to finish the job. Always obtain **written receipts** whenever money changes hands.

7. **Do not pay the bill in full** until after the work is completed to your satisfaction.

8. If possible, pay by **credit card** if the bill is for £100 or more.

9. Check the company has **public liability insurance**, and that it covers all damage to your house.

10. Make sure you receive a **written guarantee** for parts and a properly backed guarantee for the work done.

www.qualitymark.org.uk (Quality Mark) This Government-backed scheme finds Quality Mark tradesmen working in your area. Good consumer advice and links to advice sites. Tradesmen are inspected, work is guaranteed for up to six years, and there is a complaints resolution service.

www.skills-register.com (Skills Register) Good site, although limited area and trade coverage. Advertisers sign an agreement to submit to independent arbitration, have to follow a code of conduct and are expelled from the register if they breach it.

Furnishings and major household appliances

IN THIS CHAPTER YOU WILL FIND

When choosing major purchases for your home, it is important to be aware of all the options. As well as describing the features worth looking for, we offer plenty of tips to help you decide what to buy.

Baths and showers

SEE ALSO

Bathroom Manufacturers' Association, Directory p.273

BATHS

The bath you choose depends on the space available and your own taste. The standard bath is 1.7m (5ft 6in) long, but shorter baths and other shapes – such as oval and round baths, and corner baths – are also available. Whirlpool baths can be very relaxing, but take medical advice before use if pregnant or if you have a kidney complaint. There are two main kinds of bath:

Acrylic Lightweight, warm to the touch and less slippery than metal. Acryllic is stain resistant, but will scratch easily.

SEE ALSO

Care and cleaning, pp.111–112

Enamelled Pressed steel baths are coated with vitreous enamel and fired to give the hard finish; cast iron baths have a porcelain enamel (if installing a cast iron bath, make sure the bathroom floor can take the weight). Both types of enamel can be damaged by abrasive cleaners.

SHOWERS

You need to match shower to your water supply. Here are the choices that are available:

►

Bathroom fittings in
discontinued colours
Trent Bathrooms and
The Bathing Machine,
Directory pp.272 and
270

Extra-large bath
sheets
Chortex and The
White Company,
Directory pp.270 and
272

Mixer showers Wall-mounted showers that draw water from the hot water cylinder and cold water tank. These need a cold tank at least 1m (3ft) above the shower-head for sufficient water pressure. Thermostatic controls cost more than manual ones, but will prevent you from being scalded if another cold water tap is turned on.

Instant electric showers These draw water from the rising cold-water mains only and heat it on demand. They can be installed almost anywhere and are a good choice if you do not have much stored hot water. Economical, but look for a wattage of at least 8kW for an adequate flow.

Power showers These add a booster pump to a mixer to give a strong spray, and can be installed where there is insufficient pressure because the water tank is low. Power showers use a lot of water and you need a shower cabinet or fully tiled walls to prevent water damage.

Beds and guest beds

Antique brass
bedsteads
The Antique Brass
Bedstead Company
and the Bed Bazaar,
Directory p.270

BASES

Mattresses and bases should always be bought together. There are four types of bases:

Firm-edge These are not very common these days. Support springs are held in a 'box' construction and held in place by webbing running from side to side, covered by upholstery. These are usually sold with an open-coil-type mattress, and are most common on divans with legs. Edges are hard so sleeping area is reduced and you tend to sleep towards the middle, which is where bed will 'give' first.

Slatted These consist of wooden slats, generally about 10cm (4in) apart, held over parallel support rails. Top-of-the-range slatted bases have flexible fixing for extra 'give'. Choose a mattress recommended by the base manufacturer.

Solid- or platform-top These have no springs, so are solid and firm, with little 'give'. These bases should be used with a specially constructed mattress; foam may be used rather than springs. Mattress and base must be ventilated to prevent build-up of moisture. The cheapest type of base.

Sprung-edge These offer comfort right to the edge, and provide a luxurious sleeping area. They consist of an open-coil mattress unit that sits on top of a wooden platform – this acts as a giant shock absorber for a mattress, supporting it all over and increasing its durability. Often found with pocketed spring mattresses.

SEE ALSO

Dustmites, pp.237–238

Allergy-free bedding
The National Bed
Federation, Directory
p.274

MATTRESSES
Foam Worth considering if you are an allergy sufferer as foam mattresses do not contain animal-derived fillings, but bear in mind they are not resistant to dust mites. Light in weight, warm and do not need turning, so often recommended for the elderly or disabled. As a general rule, the heavier the mattress, the better the comfort. Look for latex or memory foam, which are superior and more expensive than polyurethane. Foam mattresses should always be well ventilated.

Spring interior Very popular. Springs form the central core of the mattress and are the main support layer. The thickness of the wire and the number of springs determine the firmness. In a top-of-the-range bed the number of springs used will be included in the sales literature or on the cover ▶

Duvet conversion
The Eiderdown
Studio, Directory
p.271

Duvet recovering
Givans, Directory
p.271

Special-sized bedding
Acton & Acton Ltd,
the Eiderdown Studio,
and Keys of Clacton,
Directory pp.270 and
271

label – a cheap, popular double will probably contain around 300 springs, whereas a bed at the luxury end of the market will contain over 2,500. There are three main types of spring mattress on the market:

- **Continuous springing:** one length of wire forms all the coils in the mattress, producing a three-dimensional knitted effect. These tend to be in the middle price range.
- **Open springing:** the most common type of mattress, and found in cheap to mid-priced beds. Consists of rows of waisted spring coils joined to adjacent springs by a continuous small-diameter spiral spring.
- **Pocketed springing:** has cylindrical coils individually enclosed in fabric pockets made from calico, viscose or polyester. Generally in the middle to top end of the price range. Independent pocketed springs are ideal for a double bed where occupants are very different in weight.

GUEST BEDS

Consider who will be using the bed, for how long and how often, and the space available. If you have room, a sofabed or single bed with a second bed concealed underneath is the best option, especially if the bed will be used for more than a night or two at a time. It is important to realize, however, that most are shorter than standard beds. Futons and inflatable air beds may be fine for children but are likely to be too low and unyielding for older people.

Sofabeds Check the one you choose is comfortable both as a sofa and as a bed, and that it is easy to convert.
- **The bed:** should be stable and not lift off the floor when you sit in the middle. Make sure you cannot feel the frame through the mattress and, if it's a double, that two people will not roll into the middle. Check maximum weight load.

10 TOP TIPS FOR CHOOSING A NEW BED

1. Don't be shy: **try it out** for comfort.
2. **Lie on the bed**, with your partner if it is a double, and stay there for as long as possible – bedding departments in stores are usually situated away from the main thoroughfare, to save embarrassment.
3. Ask for a **pillow** to replicate the way you will sleep on it.
4. Check **firmness** of bed by sliding your hand into the small of your back – if your hand becomes lodged, the bed is too soft; if there is a distinct gap, it is too hard. Make sure you are able to turn on to your side easily and that your shoulders and hips are comfortable.
5. Check the bed is **at least 15cm/6in longer** than the tallest occupant – if it is not long enough, the body will automatically move across the bed to sleep diagonally. Work out the ideal width by lying flat with your hands behind your head – elbows should not touch the sides or your partner.
6. Avoid shopping for beds when you are feeling **tired** – every bed you try will feel comfortable then.
7. **Read labels carefully** – the label will detail the type of filling that has been used for the mattress and base.
8. Spend as much as you can afford – there is no such thing as a cheap bed, only a lower-quality one. It is **worth paying more** for strong, durable springs, better stitching, hand tufting and firm handles, all of which contribute to longer-lasting performance. Sale buys are good value but avoid discount stores unless selling well known genuinely branded beds.
9. **Avoid second-hand** beds – they may be pre-1988, when the Furniture and Furnishings Fire safety regulations came into force.
10. **A new bed will feel strange**; expect it to take about three weeks before you are fully used to it.

■ **The sofa:** upholstery, padding and cushions should be secure, with no gaps between arms and back. Check patterns line up – inside and outside arms and arm strips should be symmetrical and central. Covers must fit well because creases accelerate wear and collect dirt. Soil-retardant finishes and removable covers are useful.

▶

WHAT SORT OF SOFA BED SHOULD YOU BUY?
Sofabeds convert from sofa to bed using one of the following mechanisms:
■ **Click-clack/lengthways fold:** box base of sofa supports metal frame and upholstery (foam or sprung), which doubles as a mattress. Frame opens out into sleeping surface. Suitable for frequent use but bed is low.
■ **Pull-out drawer:** front panel and seat of sofa pulls out like a drawer to form sleeping surface. Foam upholstery is reversed to become mattress. Sturdy but low. Suitable for occasional use.
■ **Three-fold:** seat cushions are removed and frame unfolds. Frame is metal, with a polypropylene or wire-mesh base, and high-density foam mattress. Suitable for occasional use, but mattress is thin.
■ **Two-fold:** cushions are removed and mechanism unfolds. Bed frame is metal with a wire-mesh or wooden, slatted base plus webbing. Mattress can be foam or sprung. Fine for frequent use, especially if mattress is sprung.

Concealed bed A second bed is tucked under the main bed and metal legs raise it to the same height. Can be used as a single, twin or double. Suitable for frequent use for all ages.

Futons A non-sprung mattress used directly on the floor or with a slatted base. Mattress fillings for futons are made either of cotton, which gives a firm support; a softer wool and cotton mix for medium support; or polyester, which is soft and non-allergenic.

STANDARD BED SIZES

BED	DIMENSIONS
Single	190cm x 90cm (6ft 3in x 3ft)
Double	190cm x 135cm (6ft 3in x 4ft 6in)
King	200cm x 150cm (6ft 6in x 5ft)
Super King	200cm x 180cm (6ft 6in x 6ft)

ORTHOPAEDIC BEDS

If your doctor has suggested an orthopaedic bed, go to a good department store. Be wary of advertisements that claim to make beds for individuals. Orthopaedic beds do not contain any miracle ingredients other than being firm.

TIP

If your existing base is sprung, a short-term solution is to buy a bed board which is placed under the mattress. Bed boards can, however, shorten the life of a mattress.

Central heating

SEE ALSO

Cookers, traditional ranges, p.36; CORGI, p.23; Central Heating Information Council and Solid Fuel Association, Directory pp.273 and 275

SEE ALSO

What sort of fuel is best for you? p.34

There are two main types of central heating system: 'wet' (or radiator) systems, and 'dry' warm-air systems.

GAS

All gas boilers sold in the UK must now comply with the relevant European safety standards, and should be serviced annually. All gas appliances must be installed and serviced by CORGI-registered installers. It is illegal to do it yourself or to use an unregistered fitter.

ELECTRIC

Most electric heating systems use off-peak electricity, which accumulates overnight and is stored in a heat-retaining block and programmed to give out heat later in the day. Heating is either from separate storage heaters or, in flats and small houses, a single central storage unit, with ducts or vents leading from it to the main rooms. Dry heating systems cannot be used to heat water.

▶

WHAT SORT OF FUEL IS BEST FOR YOU?

FUEL TYPE	PROS	CONS
Gas	Versatile, economical, clean	Needs chimney/flue
Electricity	Clean; easy to install	Can be expensive if house is large and you do not have modern storage heaters
LPG	Portable form of gas	Costly; needs flue/storage
Oil	Versatile	Needs flue/storage; smell
Solid fuel	Open fires	Needs flue/storage/attention

 WARNING

CARBON MONOXIDE

If carbon monoxide leaks from cooking and heating appliances, it can prove fatal. Always make sure appliances are regularly serviced by a CORGI-registered installer, and fit a BS approved and Kitemarked carbon monoxide (CO) alarm, available from your gas supplier or from SF Detection, in or near every room that contains a heating or cooking appliance.

Cookers and cooker hoods

FREESTANDING COOKERS

Although electric and gas cookers both have their pros and cons, there is little difference in overall performance.

Electric Cookers with double ovens generally have a large main oven which can be heated by fan, conventional elements or a combination of methods, and a smaller conventional oven.

- **Conventional (static) ovens:** use top and bottom elements together and produce moister results – good for slow-cooking items like fruit cakes or roasts – but get hotter at the top (zoned heating).
- **Fan ovens:** distribute heat more evenly throughout the oven

so you can cook on several shelves at once without having to swap trays around. They provide a slightly drier form of heat, but cooking is faster.

■ **Multi-function ovens:** combine conventional and fan cooking. Some models also include top element only (for browning) and bottom element only (for base-crisping foods like pizzas). Some ovens have several other cooking options to suit different types of food – when choosing, consider the type of cooking you generally do.

■ **Grills:** in electric cookers these are found in one or both ovens. Some have a half-grill option for grilling smaller items.

SEE ALSO

See also Carbon Monoxide, p.34

Gas Cooking by gas tends to produce moister food. Traditional gas cookers rely on zoned heating, so you may have to swap shelves halfway through cooking. Multifunctional gas ovens combine conventional and fan cooking.

■ **Grills:** these are either in the top oven or a separate compartment.

SEE ALSO

Electric cookers, p.34

Dual-fuel cookers Usually combine an electric oven with a gas hob, so you can have fan-oven options with the controllability of a gas hob.

RANGE COOKERS

These have either two side-by-side ovens or one extra-wide oven with an integral grill, plus a storage or warming compartment and a substantial hob. You will not, however, necessarily get more cooking space than with a conventional oven – external dimensions are larger but the ovens may be of normal size or even smaller. Check number of shelves supplied and usable space. In most ▶

cases, the hobs put range cookers in a class of their own because they are quick, powerful and versatile, and most have the advantage of including useful extras such as a wok burner, an extra-long burner for fish kettles, a griddle or barbecue plates and warming zones.

Reconditioned Agas
Phil Green and Son and Twyford Cookers, Directory p.272

Separate grills
Forneaux de France, Directory p.271

Traditional ranges (Aga-Rayburn, Bosky, Esse and Stanley) Will not only cook your food but also provide hot water and run your central heating. They cook indirectly, using stored heat rather than direct flame, so food is moister. However, because most have to be left on all the time, your kitchen can get very hot in summer. Most, except all-electric models, require a flue. Because they are made from cast iron, traditional ranges are very heavy to install. Few models have a grill, and some ovens lack precise controllability, which means favourite recipes may need adapting.

New-style range cookers Look like their traditional counterparts but are less solid and cannot heat water or run central heating. However, they are more user-friendly and temperatures are easy to regulate. Gas, electric and dual-fuel models are available with fan, static and multifunction ovens. All models have a grill, either in a separate compartment or in the oven, and installation is similar to a conventional domestic cooker. Most are available in a variety of colours or with a stainless steel finish.

Cooker features to look for

- **Automatic timer and minute minder**: allows you to programme oven to turn on and off automatically. A minute minder will also act as a timer.

- **Dual-circuit hotplate:** extends hotplate to suit size of pan.
- **Electronic thermostats:** more accurate than liquid-filled thermostats. Also look for sensors that monitor and control the oven temperature.
- **Half grill:** saves energy by heating only half the grill element.
- **Inner casing:** made from a single sheet of metal. One seam means fewer dirt traps.
- **Oven linings:** enamel linings must be cleaned manually. Self-clean (catalytic) linings burn off food splashes at high temperatures; over time they can clog up.
- **Removable grease filter:** grease on fan blades causes uneven cooking. Clean regularly.
- **Rotisserie:** a metal spit that works in combination with the grill element to brown foods. A similar effect can be achieved in a multifunction oven by using fan and grill together.
- **Slow-cook/eco setting:** (set around 90°C, gas mark ¼) allows gentle cooking of pot-roasts and tenderising of tough joints of meat.
- **Venting system to cool oven housing:** on the best built-in models, hot air is cooled to reduce discoloration and keep controls cool. Other useful features to look out for are cool-touch doors with multiple glazing, heat-reflective finishes and/or an integral cooling fan.
- **Warming/storage compartment or drawer:** to warm plates, using residual heat from the oven, or to store cookware.
- **Wok burners:** have three burners to distribute heat evenly across the bottom of the wok or large pan.
- **Zoned heating:** different heat zones operating at different levels.

▶

Compatible
saucepans
Pans, pp.93–96

HOBS

When buying a hob, check heat output specifications – some do not get hot enough for stir-frying or searing meat.

Electric glass-topped hobs There is a choice of three different type of heating system:

- **Halogen:** works by heat from bright light and is faster than radiant, but as technology improves the difference will become less marked.
- **Induction:** induction hobs heat the pan directly via a spiral copper coil beneath the glass surface, which transfers energy directly to the pan. The coil is not activated until an iron-based magnetic pan is placed on it (to check whether a pan contains iron, put a magnet on the base – if it sticks, it's fine) so the glass itself does not need to heat up before cooking starts, although it will remain warm immediately after use. Some hobs have a cooling fan, which operates after cooking is complete. Induction hobs take up more depth space than a standard hob.
- **Radiant:** has one continuous heating element, coiled in a snail shape under the glass. A faster alternative is a split element, which can be seen as a series of lines or a star pattern. Some hobs have ribbon-like elements that are ultra fine and similar in speed to split elements. Some effort is needed to maintain a polished-looking surface, and pan choice is limited.

Electric sealed hotplate The heating element is covered by a cast-iron plate. This is an unresponsive hob and one that is fiddly to clean.

Gas Fast and responsive, suitable for all pans and ideal for wok frying. Gas hobs can be dismantled completely and parts washed separately. A gas hob usually has a variety of burner ratings. Look for a 1kW for a slow simmer and 2.8kW for a fast boil. If you are not connected to the mains, most can be converted to bottled (LPG) gas.

Heat diffusers for hobs
Nisbets, Directory
p.271

Hob features to look for Expect to find the following on built-in hobs; some of these features are less common on freestanding cookers:

- **Automatic ignition:** will spark gas alight when controls are turned and pushed in.
- **Automatic switch off/time out:** heat switches off if left unattended for a long period.
- **Child-lock controls:** touch controls can be locked to prevent children altering setting or switching on hob.
- **Coated pan supports:** these are much easier to clean than bare stainless steel.
- **Dual element:** saves energy by matching the size of the element to the size of the pan – select only the inner ring for small pans, the outer or inner rings for bigger pans.
- **Electronic boil start/automatic heat reduce:** zone heats up to the highest setting then reduces after a set time to simmer. Ideal for pasta or potatoes.
- **Extended plate/casserole zone:** elongated cooking zone that can accommodate a casserole dish or fish kettle.
- **Flame failure:** if burner goes out accidentally, flame will re-light automatically.
- **Hob hot light:** shows when electric plates are still hot.
- **Power boost:** increases wattage on one or two rings by up to 800W for quick boiling of water, but reduces the wattage of zones operating on the same side by around 700W.
- **Range of heat outputs:** low to maintain a good simmer and high for quick heating.

▶

- **Removable pan supports:** can be taken apart and washed. Consider weight and sturdiness.
- **Timer:** can be set so hob will switch off automatically.
- **Ultra rapid burners:** for bringing water to the boil or frying food in a wok.

OVENS

Consider whether you need a double rather than a single oven – a second oven is ideal for warming food and plates – and whether to choose a built-in model or one that fits underneath the work surface. Single ovens have an integral grill that cannot be used at the same time as the oven, so they are not as versatile as a double oven. Built-under ovens slot under the work surface but you will have to bend in order to use the oven and grill. Double built-under ovens are smaller than built-in models.

Oven functions

- **Bottom element only:** useful for browning and crisping the base of foods. Use for quiches or pizzas.
- **Conventional cooking:** uses top and bottom elements together. Good for foods that have long cooking times such as fruit cake, which dries out more on a fan setting. Use for cooking food on one shelf.
- **Fan or fan-assisted cooking:** fan at the back distributes heat around oven for even heating of food cooked on several shelves at the same time. Ideal for batch-baking and should stop tastes and smells mingling. In theory, preheating is not needed, but baking times are shorter and results better if the oven is preheated.
- **Fan plus elements:** both fan and top and bottom heat are used. Ideal for pizzas and quiches, which need browning and a crispy base. Best if only one shelf is used.

■ **Fan with grill:** fan ensures heat from the grill is distributed evenly. Use for grilling thicker foods.

COOKER HOODS

When fitting a hood above a gas hob there should be a minimum height clearance of 65cm (26in); for an electric hob, the minimum height clearance is 45cm (18in). These measurements can vary, however, so make sure you follow the manufacturer's recommendations.

Types of cooker hood

■ **Ducted (also called extracted):** grease, steam and smells are removed from kitchen through a grease filter and extracted through a pipe to an outside wall. Very efficient, but installation expensive because of building work involved.
■ **Recirculating:** easier to install but not as efficient as filtered air is returned to kitchen. Only consider if you live in a flat or if your cooker is too far from an outside wall. Two filters are required for this cooker hood– a charcoal filter to absorb cooking smells and a grease filter.

Size and power For maximum efficiency, the hood should be the same width or wider than your hob, although in some cases a smaller hood is possible. The hood must be powerful enough to cope with the size of your kitchen. Ideally, you need a minimum of 12 air changes per hour to work in the kitchen comfortably, but the higher the extraction or recirculating rate, the more efficient the hood.

▶

OVEN CLEANING SYSTEMS

■ **Pyrolytic cleaning:** the most convenient and economical way of keeping an oven clean. It works by heating the oven to around 500°C for 1–3 hours to turn any food residue into ash. After cooling, the ash can be swept off the floor of the oven.

■ **Hydroclean (Neff only):** messier and less effective than pyrolytic cleaning, but less wasteful of fuel, this involves pouring water and detergent on the oven floor – the steam loosens dirt so you can wipe it off when it has cooled down.

■ **Self-clean (catalytic) linings:** the oven sides are treated with a special vitreous enamel that absorbs cooking spills. The linings feel rough to the touch and should not be cleaned with detergents. For best results, run the oven on a high temperature for around 30 minutes once a week to burn off any grease residue.

■ **Enamel linings:** feel smooth to the touch but also take the most work to keep clean. You will need to use an oven-cleaning product on a regular basis to prevent build-up of grease.

WHICH STYLE OF COOKER HOOD SUITS YOUR KITCHEN?

Telescopic	The most slimline design, with an extendable panel that pulls out over hob when unit is in use.
Integrated	Has a cupboard door on the front to match rest of kitchen. Opening door switches on fan; closing switches it off.
Freestanding/conventional	Can be installed against the wall or directly below wall cupboard above the hob, and usually competitively priced.
Built-in/canopy	Only visible when viewed from below as generally fitted into a specially made decorative canopy or chimney breast.
Chimney and island	Create a focal point that can be sited on its own or between wall units. Accessories include utensil rails, spice racks and splashbacks.

Dishwashers

SEE ALSO

Electrical appliances
(large), p.44

Look for features that make using the machine easier, and bear in mind that special programmes like 'delicate' are worth seeking out only if you use them regularly. If space is limited, slimline or table-top models are available.

Dishwasher features to look for

- **Anti-flooding device:** offers peace of mind. For extra protection, check when you buy machine that its inlet pipe has a leak sensor that turns off water if it floods.
- **Baskets:** should be sturdy, smooth-running and stay on, even when pulled right out. There should be enough room in the top basket for large plates and pans without obstructing spray arm.
- **Child safety lock:** prevents the door from being opened during the wash cycle.
- **Delay start:** allows you to set machine to start washing automatically after a time delay. This is useful if you subscribe to low tariff electricity.
- **Foldable or removable plate racks:** these help you make the most of mixed loads.
- **Half load:** for washing smaller quantities of crockery. On some models you can wash different types of crockery in different baskets, eg intensive in lower basket and delicate wash in top basket.
- **Hydrosensor:** alters amount of water used by monitoring how dirty water is as it is pumped from machine. Sensors identify when dishes are clean and can then automatically end the programme, saving water.
- **Pre-rinse (also called pre-wash or soak):** programme that rinses plates before washing a full load.
- **Salt and rinse-aid indicators:** remind you to refill.

▶

■ **Sturdy casing and insulating cavity between inner and outer panels:** these are features that are available on more expensive machines – will reduce noise.

ITEMS THAT ARE NOT DISHWASHER-SAFE

Aluminium pans (including hard-anodised, non-stick coated and cast aluminium)	Will react with detergent and discolour
Antique or hand-painted china	Colours will fade
Cast-iron pans	Will rust if uncoated
Cutlery with handles of bone, wood, pearl or plastic	Handles can crack, swell and distort, so check with cutlery manufacturer
Flexible plastics such as storage boxes	May distort
Lead crystal	May crack or dull
Unglazed pottery	May crack
Wooden items	Will swell and crack unless specially treated

Electrical appliances (large)

SEE ALSO

Dishwashers, p.43–44;
Freezers, p.52–53;
Fridges and fridge-freezers, p.53–55;
Tumble dryers, p.64;
Washer/dryers, p.65
and Washing machines, pp.66–67

ENERGY LABELS

All new dishwashers, freezers, fridges, fridge-freezers, tumble dryers, washer dryers and washing machines must by law carry an EU energy label.

■ Most appliances are graded from A to G. An A in the top part of the label means the model is among the most energy-efficient for that type of appliance (cutting electricity bills as well as being less damaging to the environment), while a G indicates that the machine is energy-greedy. Since 1 September 1999, all new chest freezers must be in the A-E band and all other refrigeration appliances must be in the A-C band.

■ The labels also confirm the manufacturer's name and model number (check this is the same as the model you choose to buy), and give information on energy consumption (how much electricity this particular model uses in standard tests); water consumption, conservation and efficiency; and noise levels (the lower the number, the quieter the appliance).

For more information on energy labels, ask at the store you are buying from or contact the Department for Environment, Food and Rural Affairs (DEFRA).

INTEGRATED APPLIANCES

These have special fixings that enable them to be 'hidden' behind doors that match the rest of your kitchen units, to give a uniform finish. Some can be covered by a full door; others are designed to leave the control panel exposed. Integrated appliances usually cost more than standard appliances.

Flooring

Qualitas, p.67

Care and cleaning, p.177

CARPETS

Pay as much as you can afford, but shop around as prices vary from shop to shop. Check what you are getting for your money – ask for a breakdown of fitting and accessory costs such as gripper rods, and whether extra is charged for taking up and disposing of old carpets, removing doors, etc. Durability is an important factor. To check for durability, press your hand on the pile and monitor how long it takes to spring back into shape – the faster, the better. The most durable is short, dense pile – and, if the construction is good (ie it is tightly woven, and the tufts are close together), a combination of 80 per cent wool to 20 per cent nylon.

Styles available

- **Axminster:** have complicated patterns and velvet-like cut-pile finishes and are usually made from a combination of 20 per ▶

cent nylon and 80 per cent wool – fairly hardwearing but still soft underfoot. More expensive than tufted carpets.

- **Deep pile:** luxurious and ideal for bedrooms.
- **Loop pile:** tough, hardwearing and ideal for hallways, but they can trap grit and dust in the loops so always need very thorough vacuuming.
- **Saxony:** has a longer-cut, soft-textured pile that is ideal for bedrooms and does not show marks easily.
- **Tufted:** usually the most inexpensive as they are produced quickly and in bulk. Available in plain designs and a variety of materials from 100 per cent nylon to 100 per cent wool, or a combination of the two.
- **Velvet:** luxurious and ideal for bedrooms, but avoid if you have pets as velvet will show animal fluff.
- **Wilton:** these carpets are even more expensive than Axminster as they involve a complicated weaving process and are normally 100 per cent wool.

Weights Look for the British Carpet Manufacturers Association (BCMA) label and grading scheme on British carpets, which gives details of pile fibre, construction, cleaning and room suitability.

Class 1: light use, such as bedrooms
Class 2: medium general use, such as dining areas
Class 3: heavy use in halls, living rooms and on stairs
Class 4: extra-heavy use

Fitting It is worth paying for professional fitting – a good fitter will ensure floor is properly prepared, that patterns and seams are correctly matched, that the pile is laid in the right direction, and that carpets are wrinkle-free and snug fitting. Contact the National Institute of Carpet and Floor Layers for details of local fitters.

WHICH CARPET FIBRE TO USE FOR WHICH ROOM IN YOUR HOME

FIBRE	SUITABLE FOR	PROS	CONS
Polyamide/nylon	Kitchens, play areas, bathrooms. For heavy-wear areas, look for a twisted pile nylon carpet	■ Very strong fibre ■ Durable, and if pile is dense will resist crushing ■ Keeps its colour well ■ Good economy choice ■ Rot resistant	■ Does not maintain its appearance well in low-density carpets ■ Once flattened, pile is difficult to restore ■ Cheap, untreated types can cause static shock
Polyester	Bedrooms	■ Does not fade easily ■ Warm feel	■ Cheap, untreated versions are prone to soiling ■ Once flattened, pile is difficult to restore
Polypropylene	Kitchens, bathrooms. Choose a carpet with a water-resistant backing	■ Good value ■ Non-absorbent and easy to clean ■ Colourfast ■ Low in static	■ Will flatten more easily than wool
Wool (generally blended with 20 per cent nylon for greater resilience and durability)	Heavy-duty areas such as hallways and stairs. For maximum durability look for a short, dense pile	■ Good resistance to soiling and wear ■ Soft and comfortable ■ Good insulation properties ■ Pile does not flatten easily, so retains its appearance well	■ Can rot if left wet ■ Expensive, but you get what you pay for

Underlay Good underlay is very important, especially in heavy traffic areas such as halls and stairs – it will prolong the life of your carpet, prevent dust penetrating floorboards, add comfort, and offer sound and heat insulation.

▶

IMPORTANT

Never use old underlay with a new carpet – it will carry tread patterns of the previous covering.

Stain protectors Mainly applied to synthetic carpets, as wool carpets have greater inherent stain-retarding properties. They can be applied in situ, but last longer if applied during manufacture.

HARD FLOORING

Before you can lay any new floor, you will need to check the condition of the sub-floor beneath. This should be level and free of cracks and protruding nails. Any unevenness or damp should also be dealt with before laying the new floor. Some types of flooring, such as laminates and cork, require that a waterproof membrane or padded underlay be laid under them first. You can probably take care of minor problems yourself, but more severe faults are best left to the professionals.

Brick Warm and rustic-looking, and best suited to areas such as kitchen/dining room and conservatory. Different patterns can be laid by positioning bricks at different angles, such as herringbone style.

Ceramic tiles Hardwearing, hygienic and easy to clean, but cold, hard and noisy, and may crack or chip if anything heavy and rigid is dropped on them. Ideal for kitchens, utility rooms, conservatories and bathrooms. When choosing, make sure the wear rating is suitable for the final use – eg a minimum of PEI grade 4 for heavy-duty areas, and grade 3 for bathrooms. Can fit them yourself, or use a professional tiling contractor.

Cork An excellent noise buffer, and warm and resilient underfoot. Cork tiles vary in thickness – the thicker and denser the better. Also available in strip laminate form. Ensure tiles are thick enough to withstand sanding down if wear occurs, and avoid using thin cork wall tiles as a cheaper alternative. Do not forget to budget for a sealant unless ready sealed.

Laminates Usually made from a wood composite base with a laminate surface that has been treated with an acrylic topcoat to increase resistance to wear and tear. Cheaper than wood, and available in a wide range of colours and designs. Laminate boards need to be laid on a sound, level base such as a concrete sub-floor (with acoustic boards on top), or at right angles to existing floorboards. Look for boards that click together and do not require glueing.

Linoleum (Sold under the brand name Marmoleum in the UK.) Warm, quiet and hardwearing, and will resist dents, scratches and minor burns. Made from natural materials including cork and linseed oil, it is inherently slip resistant and fade-proof, so ideal for a conservatory; it is also naturally antibacterial, so perfect for allergy sufferers. Difficult to lay, so opt for professional fitting.

Marble Marble tiles have a coolness reminiscent of the Mediterranean, and are hardwearing and easy to clean but are noisy for an indoor surface. Best fitted by a professional, and may need sealing from time to time. Very heavy – check floor is strong enough.

Metal sheet flooring Extremely durable and practical choice for kitchens and bathrooms. A metal sheet floor looks funky and modern, but can feel quite cold and uncomfortable to walk on in bare feet. While aluminium chequer-plate is the most usual choice, steel floor plate is also gaining popularity, ▶

but needs to be galvanised to stop it rusting. Look for sheeting with a thickness of at least 2–3mm.

Natural fibre floor coverings

- **Coir:** made from coconut husks, with a coarse texture. Suitable for most rooms but too scratchy for areas where you might sit on the floor – eg in a playroom.
- **Jute:** made from bark yet soft underfoot. Suitable for bedrooms and other areas where wear is light. Treat with an anti-stain protector.
- **Mixed fibres:** combines the best qualities of natural flooring with the practicality of other fibres such as wool. Suitable for use anywhere in the house.
- **Rush matting:** a hardwearing flooring similar to seagrass. Rush fibres give a smooth, flat finish that wears well, but take care with furniture legs, castors and high heels.
- **Seagrass:** woven into herringbone or basketweave designs, it is hardwearing and ideal for hallways. Slightly slippery finish makes it unsuitable for stairways.
- **Sisal:** made from a cactus-like plant, it is tough and hardwearing. Suitable for busy areas such as living rooms and hallways. Soft woven sisal is suitable for bedrooms.

SEE ALSO

Care and cleaning,
p.122

Quarry and terracotta Popular in kitchens, halls and conservatories, but noisy underfoot. Quarry tiles are very hardwearing. Can be hand-pressed, factory made or reclaimed. Terracotta tiles are porous and need careful maintenance.

Rubber Soft, warm underfoot and hardwearing, and ideal for wet areas like bathrooms and kitchens as it is water-resistant and anti-slip. Must be professionally fitted. Wide range of textures and colours available including studded and ribbed versions. Improves/hardens with age.

Slate Available in many shades and three finishes – diamond sawn (smooth, matt finish), riven (where it is naturally split, leaving a textured surface), and fine rubbed (with a light sheen). Slip resistant, even when lightly polished. Very heavy, so check floor strength.

Stone (including limestone, slate, travertine and granite)
Extremely durable and hardwearing, and perfect for heavy traffic areas such as hallways and kitchens, but can be noisy underfoot. Very heavy, so check floor strength. Works well when combined with underfloor heating. Usually sold in tile form, stone should be fitted professionally and protected with a specialist stone sealant.

Vinyl The most versatile flooring available, vinyl imitates the appearance of natural flooring while retaining a softer, warmer feel. Available in sheet or tile form. Smooth surface is easy to clean, comfortable, hardwearing and reasonably stain resistant, so ideal for kitchens, bathrooms and playrooms. Quick and easy to lay. Choose the thickest cushioned vinyl you can afford.

Wood Warm underfoot, hardwearing and easy to clean, and can be laid anywhere except in areas that are likely to get wet as wood may become slippery or absorb water and warp. Ideal for people with dust allergies. Needs to be laid over acoustic boards to help muffle sound.
- **Parquet flooring:** blocks of hardwood either loose-laid or stuck to a level base. Parquet looks wonderful and lasts for years, but is expensive.
- **Tongue and groove:** solid hardwood boards that can be sanded from time to time to keep them looking good. Lay them at right angles over existing boards or on a concrete

▶

sub-floor – you may need to trim doors. More expensive than laminate boards.

Freezers

There are two main types, upright freezers and chest freezers (more suitable for larger or awkward-shaped items). Both usually have an area for fast-freezing fresh food.

Freezer features to look for

- **Audible signal:** to warn if door has been left open, or internal temperature is too high to store food safely.
- **Childproof features:** to stop temperature of freezer being altered accidentally. Look for a temperature dial that can only be turned with a coin, buttons that have to be unlocked before settings can be changed.
- **Clear indicator lights and temperature display:** help you make sure freezer is at correct temperature.
- **Cold accumulation block:** a block that is frozen and stored in the freezer to increase length of time the freezer stays cold in the event of a power failure or breakdown.
- **Enclosed condenser plate:** will make cleaning easier as dust will not collect in it. (The condenser is a black grille, often visible at the back of the appliance – if you can see it, it is not enclosed.)

CLIMATE CLASS

When choosing a freezer, look for the 'Climate class' rating, which will help you choose the right freezer for your room. N (normal) is for a room with a temperature range of 16-32°C (61-90°F). If your room drops below 16°C (61°F) at night – or you keep your freezer in a garage, where temperatures can fall as low as 10°C (32°F) – an SN (sub normal) model might be suitable. An ST (sub tropical) model is for places between 18-38°C (64-100°F).

- **Fast-freeze:** helps keep temperature low when you add large quantities of fresh food. Some models automatically revert to the normal setting once food is frozen; others have to be switched back manually.
- **Freezer tray:** small tray at the top or bottom of the freezer, useful for freezing small items such as berries and herbs individually and for ice-cube trays.
- **Frost-free:** no need to defrost – it incorporates a heater that comes on periodically to eliminate ice and a fan that circulates cold air around the cavity. Frost-free models are slightly more expensive and some models are noisier to run than standard models.
- **Pull-out drainage spout:** allows water to be drained away more easily when you defrost the freezer. Make sure tube is high enough for a container to fit under. Alternatively, choose a frost-free model.
- **Solid drawers:** easier to pack and clean than shelves as they can be removed, and keep the cold in better than mesh drawers. Before you buy, check the drawers glide easily and that there are stops at the back.

Fridges and fridge-freezers

SEE ALSO

Replacement wire baskets
Hamster Baskets,
Directory p.268

There are two main types of fridge – larder fridges (where all the space can be used for storing fresh food) and those with an ice box compartment for storing commercially frozen food and making ice cubes. The ice box will have a star rating to indicate how long food can be safely kept in it. With a combined fridge-freezer, you will need to decide which compartment you want to be bigger, and whether you want the fridge or freezer to be on top.

▶

STAR RATINGS OF FREEZER COMPARTMENTS

Commercially frozen foods can be stored in an ice box or freezer compartment as follows.

STAR RATING	TEMPERATURE of compartment	STORAGE TIME
*	-6°C (20°F)	1 week (pre-frozen food only)
**	-12°C (10°F)	1 month (pre-frozen food only)
***	-18°C (0°F)	3 months (pre-frozen food only)
****	-18°C (0°F) or colder	6 months (pre-frozen food); can also be used to freeze fresh food from room temperature

SEE ALSO

Getting rid of things, p.229

Fridge/fridge-freezer features to look for

- **Auto defrost:** defrost water in fridge drains into a trough at back of appliance and evaporates.
- **Digital displays, indicator lights and audible signals:** allow you to monitor temperature easily. Also let you know if the door has been left open or if there is a fault with the appliance.
- **Extra storage compartments in door:** handy for items you need to keep upright or for storing smaller items that get lost on shelves and in drawers.
- **Fridge shelves that split in two:** (or are hinged) help store bottles and bulky items.
- **Humidity controls on salad, meat and cheese drawers:** these allow you to alter the airflow and temperature to help keep food fresher for longer.
- **Separate controls:** allow you to set the fridge and freezer controls independently of each other.
- **Solid drawers in freezer/glass shelves in fridge:** retain the cold better than mesh drawers and are easier to pack and clean. Check that the drawers and shelves glide easily and that there are stops at the back.
- **Vacation/holiday mode:** switches off fridge compartment but leaves freezer running while you are away.

■ **Water filters and ice-cube makers:** great for providing constant cooled filtered water and ice, but they need plumbing into the mains water supply.

American-style fridge-freezers Wider than standard fridge-freezers, but check inside to see what usable space you actually get – it can be less than you expect.

Furnishing fabrics and blinds

SEE ALSO

Fabric care and cleaning, pp.152–171

FURNISHING FABRICS

When choosing fabrics for curtains and upholstery, price and design are not the only factors. You also need to consider:

■ Which room they are to go in – eg bedroom curtains need to be opaque.
■ How hardwearing the fabric needs to be.
■ Draping characteristics – particularly for curtains.
■ Ease of cleaning – some areas, such as the kitchen, will require more frequent cleaning than others, so opt for washable fabric rather than dry-clean only.
■ Whether fabric will crease easily.
■ If the fabric is to be used for upholstery it needs to be treated with a fire retardant.

Fabric weight

Lightweight fabrics (such as some cottons and polycottons) are suitable for bathroom and kitchen curtains. In living rooms

HEM WEIGHTS
These help curtains hang properly. Sew weights into mitred corners and hem, or lay lead tape (available from specialist curtain fabric shops or John Lewis) into the hem fold and secure it at intervals.

▶

10 TIPS ON BUYING AND USING FABRIC

1. Take along a **sample** of your wallpaper, plus colour charts and upholstery swatches for colour matching.
2. Check any **pattern is printed correctly** throughout the length you require.
3. **Allow one pattern repeat** for each drop or length to ensure you join the pattern together. Small or random patterning works out cheaper because you waste less material matching repeats.
4. Always **try draping fabric** in the shop – you get a better idea of texture and effects of light on colours and patterns, and how translucent fabric is.
5. **Do not skimp** on the amount of fabric – curtains should be at least twice as wide as the window. Some washable fabrics are treated with a shrink-resistant finish – check at point of purchase. Otherwise, allow for 10 per cent shrinkage and ideally, wash fabric at least twice before making up. Ready-made curtains include 5 per cent extra for shrinkage.
6. Check fabric is **fade-resistant**. Curtains, for example, are constantly exposed to sunlight. A pattern woven into the fabric is more likely to resist fading than a pattern that is printed on.
7. Buy all the fabric you need for matching cushions etc, at the same time as your curtain fabric, as **batch colours may vary**.
8. Parallel or horizontal lines need to be aligned with walls and ceiling rather than furniture. Even apparently random patterning may have some order – stand well back and **check all the lines of pattern**.
9. To check **direction of pattern**, look at the selvedge. There may be directional arrows to guide you – otherwise, in the case of flowers, think about the natural way they would grow.
10. Prolong the life of loose covers by having two sets and changing them over now and again, and have a separate set of **removable arm covers** made for where a chair gets most wear.

and bedrooms, use lining and interlining to improve drape of curtains, insulation and light exclusion. Heavier-weight fabrics and tighter weaves offer better insulation but can be heavy to hang if lined – check curtain rail will support weight.

Linings These help the drape and general appearance of curtain fabric, and can be permanent or detachable. If lining is stitched permanently in position, dry-clean curtains otherwise the two fabrics may shrink at different rates, causing puckering. Lining also protects curtains from sunlight (which can fade and rot fabric), dust and dirt, and condensation (which can cause brown staining). Do not line curtains that need to be washed, such as those used in kitchens and bathrooms.

Stain-resistant treatments It is worth having new fabrics specially treated for stain resistance, or buying pre-treated upholstery or fabric. Treatments prevent spilt liquids being absorbed before you have time to mop them up – you still have to remove spills, but if you act quickly permanent staining will be prevented. General grime from normal use will also be slower to build up. When buying this sort of treatment, check warranty offered – some include the services of a professional cleaner. You can have existing furniture treated, but protection will not be as good as on new fabrics.

BLINDS
Ideal for small rooms as they do not take up much space; larger windows may need two or more blinds rather than one big one. Not all blinds block out the light, so check when choosing fabric and type.

Conservatory blinds Essential to reduce heat and glare, unless conservatory has reflective glass. Materials designed for conservatory use will withstand extremes of temperature and humidity without rotting or distorting, and include densely woven polyester, metal-coated acrylic and glass fibre finished with PVC. If funds are limited, just buy blinds for the roof; you could also use screens or tall plants to provide shade.

▶

WHICH STYLE OF BLIND FOR YOUR WINDOWS?

Austrian/festoon	Scalloped fabric blind that combines drapery of a curtain with the motion of a blind. Fabric should be plain and simple for maximum effect.
Roller	Moves up and down on a simple roll apparatus – simple to make and hang. Tightly woven fabrics provide the smoothest finish.
Roman	Fabric pulls up into a series of broad, flat folds. Can be made from wide range of fabrics including lightweight ones for low levels of light control.
Venetian	Suitable for minimalist interiors, bathrooms, offices. Usually metal or wood. Offer good control of light and shade, but fiddly to clean.

Kitchen units and work surfaces

UNITS

For both flat-pack and rigid units, and other kitchen components such as work surfaces, look out for the following quality assurance schemes and organisations:

■ **British Standards Institution Kitemark:** means units have been tested by the British Standards Institution and have passed

5 TIPS ON BUYING A NEW KITCHEN

1. Never accept a quote for the design and installation of your kitchen until the supplier has visited your home. Once a **complete survey** has been carried out, ensure you have a full quotation for the kitchen's installation.
2. Always **visit the showroom** before choosing your kitchen to check out the quality for yourself.
3. Do not sign anything unless you are prepared to honour your side of the contract. Some terms and conditions have **expensive cancellation clauses**. If in doubt, contact the KSA helpline.
4. Never pay a **deposit** of more than 25 per cent of the total contract value and make sure you get a written payment schedule.
5. Never pay in full until you have received delivery of your kitchen. All good kitchen retailers will allow you to **retain a portion of the cost** of the kitchen until the contract has been completed to your satisfaction.

WHICH DOOR MATERIAL FOR YOUR KITCHEN UNITS?

DOOR	CONSTRUCTION	APPEARANCE AND PRICE
Coloured/wood effect	Medium-density fibreboard (MDF) or chipboard covered with laminate, PVC or melamine.	Wide range of colours and patterns available in both matt and high gloss. Wide price range.
Wood veneer	MDF or chipboard covered with a thin layer of wood.	Looks like solid wood but is generally less expensive and more environmentally friendly (if from sustainable farmed sources). There is often less variation than with solid wood, so they give a more standard look.
Solid wood		A wide range of colours and styles, including hand-painted. Expensive – but cheaper doors, which may not have been treated properly, may discolour. Before buying, discuss the different qualities of different types of wood and how they have been treated.

stringent tests for fitness for purpose, quality and workmanship. The BSI also carries out additional tests for quality and sturdiness, ease of assembly, and how well they withstand staining and cleaning.

- **FIRA Gold Award:** means the Furniture Industry and Research Association (FIRA) has been commissioned by the manufacturer to test units and they have passed the BSI test.

SEE ALSO

Qualitas, p.67

- **Kitchen Specialists Association (KSA):** all KSA members have been trading for two years or more and are monitored regularly to make sure they continually meet the organisation's stringent criteria. The organisation also runs a consumer helpline and can offer an independent ▶

conciliation and adjudication service should a customer make a complaint against against one of the KSA members.

Features to look for in a carcass

SEE ALSO

Integrated appliances doors, p.45

- **Door hinges:** should be metal – plastic is not strong enough.
- **Drawer units:** should have full-height back panels to stop things falling down the back, and drawers should be fitted with stops so they will not fall out of the unit when opened fully. Try placing something in a drawer to test it runs smoothly with a weight inside. Runners should be metal, not plastic – they are smoother-running and will not perish.
- **Glass fronts:** should be safety (laminated) glass.
- **Interiors:** all exposed edges should be sealed – if not, chipboard panels and shelves can be weakened by moisture.
- **Shelves:** for maximum versatility, shelves in units should be adjustable.

TIP Expect a guarantee of five years to cover cabinets and worktops for problems arising from faulty materials and manufacture. Check if guarantee is valid for installation you do yourself.

WORK SURFACES

Buy the best quality you can afford. If having a worktop delivered, check its condition before signing for it – because they are large and awkward to transport, worktops are often dropped or knocked in transit.

Ceramic tiles Available either glazed or unglazed. Check tiles you choose are suitable for worktops. Tiles should be vitrified and fixed using epoxy grout. Any spills should be cleaned up immediately.

Laminates The most popular option and available in a wide range of colours, finishes and textures. Laminate worktops consist of a thin sheet of laminate on a chipboard base, and there is a great difference between the top and bottom ranges in price and quality. Most laminates will withstand temperatures of up to 180°C (360°F), while some high pressure laminates are heat resistant to 230°C (450°F). Cheaper ranges may not withstand high temperatures and become quickly damaged. It is usually worth having worktops fitted professionally.

Man-made solid surfaces (eg Corian) A composite material that is the same colour and texture throughout. A combination of an acrylic substance with added mineral particles such as silica, quartz or granite, which give strength and depth of colour and are resistant to temperatures of up to 280°C (540°F). Available in a variety of colours, and can be shaped, carved or inlaid. Joints are virtually invisible, giving a smooth and seamless finish. This sort of work surface is expensive, and can only be fitted by experts. White Corian needs vigilance to avoid staining and scratching.

Natural solid surfaces (eg granite) Look good but not very practical – you cannot have as many inlays or carved features as with a man-made solid surface, and joins may show. Surface is prone to scratches and chips. Expensive but very attractive, and cool to touch, so excellent for pastry-making. It is possible to fit a natural solid work surface yourself, but it may be more sensible to have this type of surface professionally fitted.

▶

Stainless steel Surface marks easily but the scratches blend together over time to give a uniform patina. Textured stainless steel, however, disguises marks.

Wood A hardwood worktop is a modern classic but is also high maintenance. Susceptible to damp, avoid using wood next to a butler sink, where it is difficult to form a watertight seal. To protect wood above a washing machine or dishwasher from condensation, you will need to use a special moisture-resistant paper on the underside of the work surface. Wood needs oiling regularly and can usually be sanded if scratches become too noticeable.

Sinks and taps

SEE ALSO

Care and cleaning, pp.131–132

SINKS

Although the popularity of dishwashers means sinks are used less, many households still need one that is a good size – one-and-a-half-bowl styles are the most popular choice. For an easy-to-wipe-down flush finish, choose between an integrated or undermounted design that sits level with the work surface or a top-mounted sink that is raised above the worktop. If you have plenty of space, consider a freestanding unit; if space is very tight, opt for a circular sink with no drainer. Corner sinks create more space in your kitchen.

TIP

Think carefully before you decide to do without a drainer, without having somewhere to leave dishes to dry, or a way of directing water into the sink, you will end up with water dripping on to the floor.

Ceramic Available in traditional designs such as the butler or Belfast – ideal if you need a deep, spacious sink. For a less rustic look consider more contemporary designs that are set into the worktop. Ceramic is hardwearing and durable, stain, scratch and heat-resistant, but can chip.

Composites (eg Corian) A combination of an acrylic substance with added mineral particles such as silica, quartz or granite, which give strength and depth of colour and are resistant to temperatures of up to 280°C (540°F). Sinks are fully integrated into the work surface, with no seams or joins to trap dirt. With light colours you will need to mop up spills immediately to avoid staining.

Enamel Usually enamelled cast iron or mild-steel, with a glass-like finish. Available with a matt or gloss finish, and in a range of colours. Can be vulnerable to chips and scratches.

Stainless steel The most popular material for sinks – it is resistant to high temperatures, durable and easy to clean. However, it can dull and scratch easily – scratches may show up on the shiny surface when new, but become less obvious in time. Available in different grades: 18/10 is good quality and will not distort. Stainless steel is noisy, but a vibration damper (usually a self-adhesive fibre pad) will help to keep the noise down.

TAPS

Most sink manufacturers make taps to complement their sinks. Chrome is most popular, with brass, gold, nickel, pewter, coloured and granite-effect finishes also available. Taps do not automatically fit all sinks, so check they are the correct size and reach for the sink bowl. If you choose a shallow sink, buy small taps or high ones to give clearance for filling deep vessels, and for more than one bowl, choose   ▶

swivelling mixer taps that can reach all the bowls and draining boards. Some taps are designed to be used with one hand, for people with weak grip. All water fittings and their installation must satisfy your local water supplier's by-laws, so check before installation. Some very modern tap fittings require good water pressure to work properly.

Tumble dryers

Whether you choose a condenser or vented dryer will depend on where you need to put it. A condenser can go anywhere as it does not have a hose – instead, the hot air produced is turned back into water and collected in a built-in tray. An accessible water tray will make emptying easier (some are hidden behind a plinth). Vented dryers use a hose to pass steam through a window, wall or door to the outside, so you need access to an outside wall or window. Condenser models tend to dry clothes more quickly than vented ones but cause more shrinkage and use around 20 per cent more electricity than vented dryers – they are usually more expensive too.

Timer vs sensor operation A timer dryer runs for the time you set. Sensors will dry to a set moisture level – these are useful for eliminating guesswork on timing but are not as efficient as timers for smaller loads or with fabrics of different thickness and type.

Tumble dryer features to look for
- **Anti-crease:** tumbles clothes without hot air after drying time has ended to keep them crease-free for longer.
- **Cool-down phase:** allows clothes to cool slowly, reducing shrinkage, as heater switches off for the last few minutes.

Washer/dryers

Worth considering only if you are short of space; you get better washing and drying results if you go for a separate washing machine and dryer.

- Wash times are shorter than those of a washing machine, which means clothes do not stay in contact with detergent long enough to remove stains.
- Combined machines take up to twice as long to dry clothes as a dedicated dryer.
- If you wash a larger load than the machine can dry at one time, you will have piles of damp washing to deal with – you will need to divide the load in half after washing so you do not overload the machine and cause clothes to become tangled and creased.
- After drying, clothes can feel damp even if completely dry because steam gets trapped in fibres – to prevent over-drying and reduce ironing, let load 'rest' for a few minutes before reloading dryer, to allow trapped steam to evaporate.

SEE ALSO

Washing machine features, pp.66–67

Washer/dryer features to look for

- **Anti-crease option:** continues to tumble clothes without heat after hot-air drying finishes.
- **Cool-down phase:** reduces shrinkage.
- **Reverse tumble:** helps reduce creasing.
- **Soak programme:** (up to two hours) recommended for heavily soiled items.
- **Sensor control:** allows you to specify the level of dryness on a tumble programme.
- **Timer control:** this allows you to set a specific drying time for a particular load.

▶

SHORT OF FLOOR SPACE?

If you have floor space for only one unit but do not want to go for a washer/dryer, you can stack a tumble dryer on top of your washing machine. Most manufacturers sell a stacking kit, consisting of a metal frame that fits on top of the washing machine. To ensure you get a proper fit, it is a good idea to match the frame to your washing machine, but most dryers are a standard size so you do not necessarily have to buy the same brand of dryer to stack them up.

Washing machines

TIP

It is worth looking for a high energy-efficiency rating – these days, energy efficient washing machines are not necessarily any more expensive. You will save money on running costs and your machine should last longer.

SEE ALSO

Electrical appliances,
(large) p.44

Washing machine features to look for

- **Anti-crease cycle:** periodically tumbles clothes up to 30 minutes after washing.
- **Bracket hinges:** allow the door to open 180° for easy loading. Curved metal plate hinges open to just 90°.
- **Counterbalances:** usually a concrete slab in the top or base of the machine designed to reduce vibration during spinning. On expensive models, these cradle the drum, reducing noise and wear.
- **Drip dry/no spin:** useful for delicate items as it completes a wash programme without the final spin.
- **Electronic door-open button:** mid- to low-price models use a mechanical spring that can wear out.
- **Freshen-up option:** a rinse with conditioner, which is suitable for delicate clothing.
- **Fuzzy logic:** sensors that monitor the wash cycle (in mid- to high-price models) to ensure you get optimum wash performance. Balance controls or soft suspension systems

detect and correct load imbalances, reducing noise and minimising wear and tear.

- **Gentle/hand/silk washes:** reduce amount of agitation in the wash to suit delicate items.
- **Memory function:** recalls additional options selected the last time a programme was run.
- **Refresh programme:** washes lightly soiled delicate fabrics for a short time at 30°C.
- **Self-diagnosis display:** automated troubleshooting guide on the control panel to help overcome minor problems without the need to call out a service engineer.
- **Soak:** recommended for heavily soiled and stained items. Clothes are steeped in water for up to two hours before being machine-washed.
- **Stainless steel heating element:** this will last longer than the usual mild steel, and will resist limescale.
- **Stainless steel ribs on inner drum:** plastic ribs can become damaged when washing items with heavy zips and buttons, which would then snag delicates and pull woollens.
- **Starch programme:** this separately starches, softens and conditions wet washing.
- **Super/stain/intensive wash:** a heavy-duty programme suitable for heavily soiled washing.
- **Thick inner drum:** drum, springs and heavy-duty bearings need to be robust to withstand high spin speeds. Rap it sharply with your knuckles – the deeper the sound, the thicker the drum.

QUALITAS FURNISHING STANDARDS

Qualitas is the furniture industry's standards body, which offers a conciliation and adjudication service to resolve disputes between consumers and its members, who are retailers of all types of furniture and furnishings, including carpets and fitted kitchens and bathrooms. Look for the Qualitas logo in stores and on promotional material.

Buying paint

HOW TO WORK OUT HOW MUCH PAINT YOU NEED

1. Measure height and width of each wall, rounding each measurement up to the nearest 10cm (4in). Multiply each wall's height and width together to find the area of each wall. Add the areas of the walls together (A).
2. Measure height and width of any doors, windows and other features to be left unpainted. For each feature, multiply the height by the width to find the area. Add areas of these features together (B).
3. Subtract B from A to give area to be painted (C).
4. Divide C by the covering capacity of the paint (see above; this figure is also usually printed on the paint can). This will give you the number of litres you require for one coat of paint.
5. Multiply number of litres needed for one coat by the number of coats to be applied.

PAINT COVERAGE AND DRYING TIMES*

TYPE OF PAINT	Area covered per litre	Touch dry	Re-coatable
Matt vinyl emulsion	12–14sq m / 129–151sq ft	2hrs	4hrs
Silk vinyl emulsion	12–14sq m / 129–151sq ft	2hrs	4hrs
Soft sheen emulsion	13–15sq m / 140–161sq ft	2hrs	4hrs
Solid emulsion	11–13sq m / 118–140sq ft	2hrs	4hrs
One-coat emulsion	10sq m / 108sq ft	2hrs	4hrs
Flexible emulsion	7–9sq m / 75–97sq ft	2hrs	4hrs
Textured emulsion	5–7sq m / 56–75sq ft	2hrs	4hrs
Water-based satin	14–16sq m / 151–172sq ft	2hrs	4hrs
Eggshell**	15–17sq m / 161–183sq ft	12hrs	16hrs
Liquid gloss	16–17sq m / 172–183sq ft	12hrs	16hrs
Non-drip gloss	10–12sq m / 108–129sq ft	1–3hrs	5–6hrs***
Water-based gloss	14–16sq m / 151–172sq ft	2hrs	4hrs
Self-undercoat gloss	10–12sq m / 108–129sq ft	2hrs	4hrs
Undercoat	15–17sq m / 161–183sq ft	8hrs	12hrs
Masonry paint	6–10sq m / 65–108sq ft	1hr	4hrs

*   Coverage varies with the brand and absorbency of the surface. Times depend on moderate, dry conditions
**   Solvent-based
*** Normally only one coat required

 SEE ALSO Painting problem solver, p.226

Buying wallpaper

WALLPAPER QUANTITIES

Standard rolls of wallpaper measure about 10.05m (33ft) long by 530mm (21in) wide, but American and continental sizes may differ. The following chart is based on standard wallpaper.

Wall height from skirting	Distance round room (including doors and windows)																	
Feet	30	34	38	42	46	50	54	58	62	66	70	74	78	82	86	90	94	98
Metres	9	10	12	13	14	15	16	17	18	19	21	22	23	24	26	27	28	30
2.15–2.30m (7–7½ft)	4	5	5	6	6	7	7	8	8	9	9	10	10	11	12	12	13	13
2.30–2.45m (7½–8ft)	5	5	6	6	7	7	8	8	9	9	10	10	11	12	12	13	13	14
2.45–2.60m (8–8½ft)	5	5	6	7	7	8	9	9	10	10	11	12	12	13	14	14	15	15
2.60–2.75m (8½–9ft)	5	5	6	7	7	8	9	9	10	10	11	12	12	13	14	14	15	15
2.75–2.90m (9–9½ft)	6	6	7	7	8	8	9	10	10	11	12	12	13	14	14	15	15	16
2.90–3.05m (9½–10ft)	6	6	7	7	8	8	9	10	10	11	12	12	13	14	14	15	15	16
3.05–3.20m (10–10½ft)	6	7	8	8	9	10	10	11	12	13	13	14	15	16	16	17	18	19

Ceilings: to calculate the number of rolls required, work out the area in square metres and divide by five.

SEE ALSO Wallpaper problem solver, p.227

Small electricals and other equipment

IN THIS CHAPTER YOU WILL FIND

Here's what to look for when buying kitchen equipment, items for the garden, music systems and televisions, as well as helpful tips and advice on getting the best out of your purchases.

Breadmakers

If you love the taste and aroma of freshly baked bread but do not have time to knead the dough, a breadmaker will do all the work for you. Just load all the ingredients into the bread pan, close the lid and switch on. The machine will automatically mix, knead, prove and bake bread – but it can take anywhere from 3–4 hours to produce a light, white loaf with a good flavour and 3–5 hours for wholemeal. A loaf will also cost almost twice as much as a similar supermarket loaf – although you do have the advantage of being able to control exactly what you put in it (essential if on a special diet).

Kitchen equipment for the disabled
The Disabled Living Centres Council, the Disabled Living Foundation and Ricability, Directory, pp. 273 and 275

Breadmaker features to look for

- **'Add extra ingredient' beep:** (or a dispenser that automatically adds ingredients to dough at right time) – essential for making speciality breads with fruit and nuts.
- **Choice of loaf size and crust colour:** to make different loaves.
- **Delay timer:** lets you programme your breadmaker up to 18 hours in advance, so you can pre-set it and wake up to the smell of freshly-baked bread.
- **Extended-bake facility:** lets you cook loaf for longer if you prefer it crisper and darker.
- **Viewing window:** lets you see how loaf is progressing, but if there isn't one you can open lid without spoiling loaf.

▶

5 TOP BREADMAKER TIPS

1. Bread is best eaten within **two or three days** of baking. Store unused bread at room temperature, wrapped tightly in a sealed plastic bag or in a covered container. For longer storage (up to one month) wrap well and freeze.
2. It's a good idea to start with the **manufacturer's recipes** supplied with the breadmaker until you get the hang of using the machine.
3. Whichever recipe you use, always **add the ingredients in the precise order** specified by the manufacturer.
4. Most breadmakers offer a **range of programmes** to cook speciality breads, cakes and jam. Most also have the option to make dough for rolls, bagels, pasta and pizza, which you can then shape and bake either in your oven or in the breadmaker using the bake-only facility, if it has one.
5. You will need to use **strong plain flour** rather than ordinary plain or self-raising flours, which do not contain enough gluten (the protein that helps the dough keep its shape and gives bread its structure). You will also need sachets of dried yeast, usually called Fast Action or Easyblend/Easybake yeast. If type and quantity of yeast is not specified, check with manufacturer – it is essential for good results.

Coffee machines

CAPPUCCINO/ESPRESSO MACHINES

It's worth paying as much as you can afford if you want to make the kind of cappuccino or espresso coffee served in coffee bars. Machines generally take little time to make their first cup of coffee, but you have to empty grounds after each cup. Some manufacturers use capsules, which are less messy to use but work out more expensive than ground coffee; other makers try to reduce the nuisance at the other end of the operation by including their own grinders.

- **Pump-operated:** produce greater pressure than steam ones, resulting in better-flavoured coffee and giving that authentic 'crema' layer (see p.74).
- **Steam-operated:** dispense only four cups before needing to

be refilled, take longer to brew, and have to be allowed to cool before you can refill them.

Cappuccino/espresso machine features to look for

■ **Automatic milk-frothing device:** fits on steam/hot water nozzle to heat and froth milk before dispensing it into jug or cups via a flexible tube.

■ **Brewing head:** nozzle through which brewed coffee passes into jug or cups.

■ **Coffee press:** flat disc that compacts ground coffee. Water takes its time filtering through coffee, giving a strong and very flavoursome brew.

10 TIPS FOR MAKING A PERFECT CUP OF COFFEE

1. Arabica and robusta are the type main types of **coffee bean** used for espresso. Arabica tends to be milder and more aromatic, while blends of arabica and robusta have more body and a stronger flavour.

2. Use **dark-roasted** fine-ground coffee, allowing 7g per cup – increasing amount of coffee makes it thicker, not stronger. Press grounds down firmly in filter to allow water to extract the full flavour.

3. To make a **good cappuccino**, use equal quantities of espresso and hot frothed milk, served in a 100-175ml (4-6fl oz) cup. Add a dusting of cinnamon or chocolate powder.

4. Always use cold, semi-skimmed milk for ease of **frothing**.

5. Use a **metal jug** taller than it is wide.

6. **Do not let milk boil** – stop heating once jug is too hot to hold comfortably.

7. Once frothed, tap jug down on to worktop and **swirl milk** around until it becomes shiny and 'stiffens' to form a dense foam.

8. Use coffee from **vacuum-sealed packs** within two weeks of opening.

9. Freshly ground coffee needs to be consumed within a week, though you can extend its life for a few days by **storing** it in the fridge in an airtight container. Beans keep for up to four weeks, up to two months in a freezer.

10. Choose individually foil-wrapped capsules to ensure **freshness**.

▶

- **Coffee volume selector:** allows you to adjust amount of water used.
- **Crema:** creamy thick layer on top of coffee, characteristic of a good espresso.
- **Cup adaptor:** plastic nozzle that allows you to fill two cups at the same time.

FILTER COFFEE MACHINES

Many machines come with permanent nylon filters – traditional paper filters are less messy as they are thrown away complete with grounds, but they do tend to give coffee a slightly papery flavour. Tank size is the best guide to capacity as cup sizes vary between manufacturers. Most models have a hotplate, but you should drink the coffee within 20 minutes or it will become overheated and bitter. Stir before serving as first drops will be stronger than last. Water can affect flavour as well so use fresh, cold tap water or try filtered or bottled water.

Filter coffee machine features to look for

- **Drip stop:** lets you remove jug during brewing without any coffee dripping through. Brewing process continues when jug is replaced.
- **Removable water tank:** can be taken over to the sink for the ease of filling.
- **Strength selector:** lets you adjust speed at which water trickles through and control strength of coffee.
- **Water tank gauge:** gives a more realistic idea of how many cups can be brewed than markings on jug.

5 TOP TIPS FOR PERFECT DEEP-FRYING

1. Use **good-quality oil** such as sunflower, groundnut or corn. For safety when cooking, avoid mixing together different types of oil or fat.
2. **Never overfill** the basket with food as this stops food being cooked through and browning evenly.
3. Fry precooked food on a higher **temperature** than raw.
4. Always make sure food is **as dry as possible** before frying, to minimise spitting and bubbling – dry on kitchen paper if necessary.
5. **Filter cooled oil into a plastic bottle** after use and re-use next time. Use fresh oil every 8-10 frying sessions.

Deep-fat fryers

Electric fryers are thermostatically controlled, so oil cannot overheat and will not make contact with a naked flame.

SEE ALSO

Getting Rid of Things, Cooking oils, p.229

Deep-fat fryer features to look for
- **Drainage tube:** allows oil to be emptied easily.
- **Filter (locking-lid models only):** sits in lid, reduces frying odours.
- **Safety cut-out:** switches off appliance if it starts to overheat.

WHICH TYPE OF DEEP-FAT FRYER FOR YOU?

TYPE	PROS	CONS
Stainless steel (without a lid)	■ Easy to use and clean ■ Generally more stylish ■ Easier to see when food is cooked	■ Higher external wall temperatures ■ Open frying allows frying odours to escape, so more smelly ■ Needs more oil
Locking-lid models (with a lid and filter)	■ Cooler wall temperatures ■ Used with lid on, so safer and less smelly ■ Needs less oil	■ Often more difficult to clean as parts are not all removable or washable ■ Cannot see when food is cooked without opening lid

Electric kettles

As they are used so often, kettles do need to be replaced frequently. The biggest cause of failure in kettles is limescale in water attaching itself to the heating element – as the layer of scale thickens, the time the kettle takes to boil increases. In the latest models, the heating element does not come into contact with water as it is hidden beneath a limescale-resistant metal disc (usually stainless steel).

 TIP

For rapid boiling, choose a kettle with a 'fast boil' or powerful 3kW heating element.

Electric kettle features to look for
- **Cord storage in base unit.**
- **Limescale filter in spout:** it should also be easy to remove, clean and replace.
- **Mark-resistant surface.**
- **'On' light.**
- **Plastic lining (on metal kettles):** to help prevent external temperature going over 90ºC (194ºF).
- **Water gauge or viewing window:** to avoid over- or under-filling.
- **360° swivel connector base:** so you can replace kettle from any angle.

Food preparation machines

BLENDERS

Jug Useful for making smooth soups, mayonnaise, batter and milkshakes and for chopping nuts, making breadcrumbs and crushing ice. Some blenders also have a mill attachment for grinding coffee beans. If possible, try out the blender before you buy – you will find that most are noisy to use and some have lids that are difficult to remove. Do not assume that a higher wattage automatically means a better blender. Measurements on the goblet are not always reliable either. For easier cleaning, look for a blender with a removable blade that is dishwasher safe.

Stick Electrically operated hand-held stick-style blenders with a small blade at the base. Useful for liquidising and puréeing foods. With care, some can also be used to process hot foods (look for one with a metal shaft).

FOOD MIXERS

A freestanding food mixer is the best type of food preparation machine for making cakes, pastries and bread – they take all the effort out of kneading doughs and whisking egg whites. Cheaper models are less effective at combining ingredients as they use a different action to more expensive mixers – their bowls and whisks rotate, whereas on more expensive machines the attachment shaft rotates in a different direction from the beaters, resulting in a more aggressive action.

FOOD PROCESSORS

Ideal if you frequently make family-sized portions of things like coleslaw, soup and mayonnaise – they take all the effort out of slicing, grating, mixing and chopping. Some will whisk egg whites and mix cakes reasonably but results are unlikely to be as good as with a food mixer.

 If you have only the occasional carrot or onion to slice, you would probably be better off investing in a good set of kitchen knives instead – these are easier to clean and store ▶

5 TIPS FOR SAFE FOOD PREPARATION
1. Let food **cool slightly** before processing as splashes can scald.
2. Always **handle blades carefully**. Make sure they have completely stopped spinning before touching them.
3. **Wash blades and cutting attachments individually** to reduce risk of injury.
4. **Never force** food through the feed chute (the opening in lid of processor for inserting ingredients when machine is operating) – and never use your hands.
5. Store blades and cutting attachments in **protective packaging**.

than the typical processor with its range of blades, discs and other attachments.

Food processor attachments to look for

- **Dough hook or plastic dough tool:** a must if you want to make your own bread. You could use the metal chopping blade instead, but it cuts through dough and gives a gluey mix.
- **Juice extractor/citrus press:** will save you buying a separate machine if you enjoy fresh juice.
- **Liquidiser goblet:** useful if you like to make your own soup or want to prepare fresh baby food because it purées to a smoother consistency.
- **Metal whisk:** ideal for whisking up perfect sponges and perfect also for whisking egg whites.
- **Mini or midi bowls:** fit inside main bowl and are ideal for preparing herbs, nuts and baby food.
- **Speed settings:** some models have one speed designed to cope with all food preparation, but sometimes it is useful to have a slower speed to give you more control. Go for a model with a couple of speeds – slower for slicing and faster for whisking, mixing, chopping and puréeing, plus a pulse mode, which gives a short burst at high speed.

MINI PROCESSORS

Consist of a bowl with a sharp blade, which often fits under a motor unit. Some come with accessories such as grating and slicing discs. Suitable for processing small quantities, like baby food, nuts or herbs.

Garden equipment

SEE ALSO

Additional costs for patio heaters and gas barbecues, p.84

BARBECUES

Consider how often you will use the barbecue and what you will be cooking on it. If you are intending to cook large items, such as a whole chicken, choose a barbecue with a lid, that will reflect heat back on to the food. Open barbecues without lids have a grill rack that sits over the heat source and can be lowered and raised, depending on the strength of the heat and the food you are cooking. Open barbecues are suitable for cooking steak, chops, sausages, burgers and chicken portions. Griddle plates are featured on some open barbecues. These are good for searing meat before cooking through on the grill.

IMPORTANT

With all types of barbecue, check the construction is sturdy and designed for stability.

Charcoal fired A simple low-cost open-grill charcoal barbecue is fine for sausages and burgers. For regular barbecuing, choose the more expensive kettle type (with a domed lid), which allows the slower, more thorough cooking needed for thick cuts of meat or poultry.

Charcoal barbecue features to look for

■ **Charcoal rack and ash catcher:** makes for easier cleaning up after you have finished barbecuing.

■ **Choice of grill heights:** a must on a lid-less grill.

■ **Side or front shelf:** for tools and condiments.

Gas Most gas models come flat-packed and assembly can be painstaking, but you don't have to wait long to get cooking – just 10 minutes while you preheat. Most use a layer of briquettes to distribute heat; cast-iron briquette plates are designed to reduce flare-ups, but the briquette material makes little difference – it depends more on how the briquettes are arranged and their distance from the heat source. Most barbecues use butane gas. For safety, store cylinders outdoors and replace hoses and regulators every two years.

Gas barbecue features to look for

■ **Automatic or manual ignition:** to light gas burner, turn control knob or press a separate button together with control knob.

■ **Briquettes:** help distribute heat from gas burners. Lava rock briquettes are the most common kind – they absorb fat from foods, so burn for longer if they catch light. Ceramic briquettes are denser than lava rocks, so they absorb less oil during cooking. Replace both types of briquette every five years. With a cast-iron briquette plate the food drips sit on the surface and burn off quickly – they don't need to be replaced.

■ **Charcoal rack:** charcoal is placed on wire racks to burn. Simply lift out to empty coals after cooking.

■ **Drip-collection cup/pan:** small metal cup for collecting any cooking deposits.

■ **Drip tray or ash-collecting tray:** tray for catching cooking deposits and ash.

■ **Griddle plate:** solid or ridged cast-iron plate. Sear meat and cook thick items on flat griddles; ridged types give food an authentic chargrilled appearance.

- **Side burner:** similar to a gas burner on a hob, designed for heating soups and sauces.
- **Spit:** long metal skewer suitable for cooking thick pieces of meat such as a whole chicken or leg of lamb.
- **Warming rack:** smaller rack above main grill for keeping cooked food warm.
- **Windshield:** shields barbecue from wind to prevent flame going out. In covered barbecues, lid acts as windshield.

LAWNMOWERS

Battery (cordless) Ideal if garden is an awkward shape as there is no mains cable to watch for. As flexible as petrol mowers but easier to start and maintain. Not good for long grass and only about 45 minutes' cutting time per charge.

WHICH CUT IS BEST FOR YOUR LAWN?

MOWER	DESCRIPTION	RESULTS
Cylinder	Series of rotating blades that cut grass with a scissor-like action against a fixed lower blade.	Gives a high-quality result with a traditional 'bowling green' finish, but needs a lot of maintenance.
Hover	Single metal or plastic blade rotates horizontally at high speed. Fan beneath hood creates an air cushion, making hover 'float' above grass.	Mowing in a straight line can be difficult, but mower is light and easy to manoeuvre, especially across uneven areas.
Rotary	Blade rotates horizontally at high speeds, cutting grass with a scythe-like action. Wheels raise mower above lawn and some have rollers to leave a traditional striped finish.	Gives a reasonable cut and good for all-purpose lawns and overgrown grass.

Electric Good for small to medium gardens as they are lightweight and need little maintenance. Best suited to square or rectangular gardens with no awkward areas, where mowing is no more than 60m (200ft) from power socket.

 IMPORTANT Always plug an electric lawnmower in via an RCD (residual current device, from hardware stores) to avoid risk of electric shock if you accidentally cut through the cable.

Petrol Good choice for larger gardens as they do not need to be plugged in. Require more maintenance and are generally noisier and heavier than battery or electric mowers. Self-propelled petrol mowers make much lighter work of cutting grass.

Lawnmower features to look for

- **AutoMatic Drive System:** similar to 'self propelled' (see below), but you can control speed of mower to suit your own pace by amount of pressure applied on handle.
- **Cable restraint:** special clip that slides across handle frame, to keep flex out of the way.
- **Cutting height:** lets you adjust height of cutting blade depending on length of grass.
- **Cutting width:** refers to blade width of mower. A larger width is better for big gardens as you need to mow fewer lengths. Medium gardens (27–120sq m/290–1300sq ft) need a cutting width of around 30cm (12in).
- **Plastic safety blade:** cuts grass but, unlike metal, won't cut cable if you run over it.
- **Rear roller:** produces stripes on lawn for a classic 'bowling green' effect.
- **Recycler facility:** instead of collecting grass in grass box, grass is chopped and forced back into lawn to 'feed' it.

- **Roto-Stop:** allows you to empty grass box while engine is running, and lets you disengage mower's blade so you can turn corners without scalping lawn.
- **Safety key:** special overload protection fuse featured on battery mowers. Mower will not work unless fitted.
- **Self-propelled:** mower is power-driven to make it easier to push and manoeuvre, but you cannot control speed.
- **Striping flap:** works like a rear roller to produce 'bowling green' stripes on the lawn.

PATIO HEATERS

These can be either gas or log-burning. Gas models are cleaner and easier to light, and higher wattage models heat a wide area. However, their appearance and size can dominate a garden. Wood-burning models add more ambience but can be smoky, take longer to light and give out less heat. Most heaters are flat-packed for home assembly, and as the average model has around 32 parts, this can prove to be quite difficult. If you can't face putting the heater together yourself, check whether the supplier offers an assembly service.

5 PATIO HEATER SAFETY TIPS

1. Look out for an **anti-tilt device**, which cuts heater off if moved from an upright position, and never move a patio heater when alight.
2. Choose a model with a **flame failure device** that cuts off gas if heater goes out.
3. Patio heaters are for **outdoor use only**. The combustion products leaving the heater are very hot and could cause a fire inside a tent or marquee. Never position heater too close to an umbrella or overhead trellis, and only use under an awning if manufacturer's instructions say you can.
4. Stand heater in a **sheltered area** to prevent it blowing out. Most heaters can't cope with winds much above 10mph/16kmph (a strong breeze).
5. Never leave a patio heater **unsupervised**.

▶

ADDITIONAL COSTS FOR PATIO HEATERS AND GAS BARBECUES

■ **Bottled gas:** on average, a cylinder lasts 18–22 hours, depending on heat output. You will also have to pay a hire charge for your first cylinder, as you won't have an empty one to exchange.

■ **Regulator:** controls gas supply to heater, but not many patio heaters are supplied with one, so double-check when you buy. If a flexible hose connects regulator to heater inlet, check it every time gas cylinder is replaced. If it shows signs of cracking or splitting, replace with a new one manufactured to BS3212 type 2.

■ **Servicing:** patio heaters and gas barbecues should be serviced at the start of every season by a CORGI-registered gas fitter (see p.23).

Patio heater features to look for

■ **Canopy shape:** shape of aluminium canopy on top of heater is important – a wider canopy with a rim gives a good level of wind protection and helps direct heat downwards.

■ **Gas cabinet:** if you have children, choose a lockable cabinet so they cannot turn on the gas. It should have an emergency access hatch in case you need to turn off gas quickly.

■ **Heat output:** you need at least 7kW, which should be enough to give a 4m (13ft) circle of heat. Low-priced heaters rated under 7kW are not effective.

■ **Heat settings:** look for high and low settings. High warms up the area when heater is first turned on; low setting will keep temperature at a comfortable level.

SUN LOUNGERS

A quality lounger should give years of service, while a cheap one may only last a summer. Most quality garden furniture comes with a one-year guarantee and advice on whether it can be left outside permanently. In general, loungers with fixed fabric cushions cannot be left outside and hardwood furniture can be left outside, although wood will fade to a silvery colour unless you restore it twice a year with teak oil.

WHICH MATERIAL IS BEST FOR YOUR GARDEN FURNITURE?

Bamboo	Lightweight but strong, and often combined with rattan for a colonial look. Bamboo is weather-resistant but loungers made from a combination of bamboo poles and woven rattan or bamboo strips will suffer if left out in the rain.
Brushed aluminium	Often used with teak or other hardwoods, or with moulded ply or Lucite (a transparent thermoplastic material formerly known as Perspex) in some modern designs. Hardwearing, it won't rust and can be left outside all year.
Hardwood	Tropical hardwoods such as teak, iroko and balau are most commonly used for garden loungers. Before you buy, make sure: ■ it is made of solid wood, not a veneer that can peel ■ timber has been kiln-dried and is furniture grade – both factors have an effect on stability and durability ■ timber comes from a sustainable source – destruction of rainforests for hardwood is a real concern. The Forest Stewardship Council registered trademark is a good guide, although not all companies utilising wood from sustainable sources use it ■ screws and other fixings are made from rustproof brass
Stainless steel	Combined with other materials, which form the seating. Lightweight, hardwearing and won't rust.
Synthetic resin	Hardwearing blend of polystyrene and minerals, synthetic resin usually comes in white, green or brown. Frost- and rustproof so you can leave frames outside all year. Cheaper resin chair frames can fade and scratch, while better quality models will generally age fairly well.
Tubular steel	Used for lower-cost recliner chairs and simple sun loungers. Frame will rust unless it has a good quality lacquered waterproof coating.

Cushions Most wooden and some resin loungers are sold with a cushion as an optional extra. Although cushions are usually covered in acrylic fabric that is hardwearing, rotproof and mouldproof, it will still need protecting from wet weather.

▶

5 THINGS TO CONSIDER WHEN BUYING A LOUNGER

1. Can you get in and out of the chair easily? If you have back or knee problems, a low lounger can be difficult and painful to use. **Better choices** may be a more upright style with a footstool, or a steamer chair that is a good height from the ground, with arms to make getting up and down easier.
2. Is the chair-back mechanism easy to move? You should be able to **adjust lounger safely** while sitting in it.
3. Does back adjust to the **right position**? If you like to sunbathe, adjustment to flat or near-flat is probably essential. If you like to read while you tan, you will need a back that adjusts to semi-upright.
4. Can lounger be left outdoors in winter? If not, do you have enough storage space? Does lounger fold for easy **storage**?
5. Is it easy to **move around**? Wooden loungers are heavy and can be very awkward to manoeuvre. Wheels make the job easier, but try them out before you buy.

 IMPORTANT Cushions should not be left in an outdoor shed in winter as mice may cause damage to the fabric and filling.

Ice cream machines

Luxury brands of ice cream are expensive, but you can cut the cost in half at home with the help of an ice cream maker. You will know exactly what has gone into your ice cream – and you can experiment with your favourite flavours and ingredients. Making ice cream by hand is hard work; with a machine there's a cooling bowl to do the freezing and a paddle that lifts and churns mixture as you pour it in. Choose between a cheaper freeze-first model or a more sophisticated self-freezing machine – whichever you choose, you'll get a soft, creamy ice cream within 40 minutes.

Freeze-first machines Consist of an insulated bowl that has a coolant within its double wall, and a motorised paddle that rotates. Bowl must be kept in a three- or four-star freezer for

5 TOP ICE CREAM MAKING TIPS

1. Always add ingredients (preferably pre-chilled) **while paddle is rotating**, otherwise you will get a crust of solid ice cream around base and sides.
2. Watch **sugar content** of recipe – too little sugar and mixture will harden too quickly and stop paddles from rotating, but too much will be overpowering (try 25g/1oz sugar per egg yolk).
3. If adding **alcohol**, wait until mixing has nearly finished because it will slow down the freezing process.
4. Home-made **ice cream** is best eaten within a week if made from raw ingredients, and within two weeks if made from cooked ingredients (custard-based).
5. **Sorbets** will last from one to two weeks.

up to 22 hours, depending on the model, before use.

Self-freezing machines More sophisticated models that contain their own compressor (like a mini freezer) and have a motorised paddle so they can churn and freeze at the same time. A good choice if you make ice cream regularly.

Irons and ironing boards

STEAM IRONS

If you live in a soft-water area and don't do a huge amount of ironing, you won't have to pay much for your iron as you won't have problems with scale build-up. Paying more will buy you a higher steam output for quicker crease removal, but you'll need to refill the tank more often.

To help iron glide across fabric better, try using a silicone spray such as Dylon Easy Iron.

Which soleplate? The soleplate (the hot base of the iron) can be made of aluminium, chrome, stainless or brushed (matt) ▶

steel, non-stick or ceramic coated metal. It's a matter of preference, but ceramic-coated ones glide most easily over a wide range of fabrics. Stainless steel soleplates are durable, but tend to drag slightly. A non-stick soleplate scratches easily and is the least effective.

Steam generator irons These have a separate water tank, attached to the iron by its flex and a cord through which the steam passes. Most expensive, but with a potentially far longer life, especially in hard-water areas. High steam output means speedier ironing, though not necessarily better results. These irons are lighter to use than a standard iron because the water tank is separate and, because the tank is over twice the size, you don't have to refill as often. But they are bulky to use and store, and you will still need to descale the tank.

Steam iron features to look for

- **Anti-drip system:** stops steam production at low temperatures to prevent water dripping out of base onto your ironing.
- **Anti-scale devices:** prevent limescale blocking holes in soleplate and furring up water tank and steam chamber. These include built-in filters that reduce limescale build-up, granules or removable cartridges that absorb mineral deposits from water (must be changed every few months), or removable valves that attract scale from water tank.
- **Safety cut-out:** switches off iron automatically if left unused for a certain number of minutes.
- **Self-cleaning facility:** forces water and steam through holes in soleplate to flush out any mineral deposits.

IRONING BOARDS
Look for ease of opening and closing, stability, weight and board size and shape. If necessary, make sure the board is

suitable for use with a steam generator iron – not all are.

Ironing board features to look for

- **Curved legs:** enables chair to fit underneath.
- **Fan assisted:** incorporates fan that sucks steam away through the board, to improve ironing efficiency. Also for creating fresh creases or reinforcing existing pleats.
- **Mesh top:** designed for use with a steam iron, allowing steam to pass through, rather than leaving ironing damp.
- **Squeeze-grip lever:** operates height adjustment.

Juice extractors

Unless you have a glut of fruit or vegetables, you may not save money by making your own freshly squeezed juice. The texture may be thinner than shop-bought varieties, and the colour will be different – apple juice may be brownish and tomato is pink. Expensive models tend to be more solidly built than cheaper ones.

5 TIPS FOR MAKING PERFECT JUICE

1. Use **fresh, well-ripened** fruit and vegetables and always wash them very thoroughly before placing them in the juice extractor.
2. **Avoid using very fibrous fruits** such as rhubarb as they do not generate much liquid and also make the juicer far more difficult to clean.
3. Peel thick-skinned fruit and vegetables, such as melon, pineapple, kiwi and beetroot. Roll up leaf vegetables tightly and stone fruit such as cherries and peaches. Chop fruit and vegetables into **suitably sized pieces** for your juicer's feed tube.
4. Store freshly made juice in an **airtight container** in the fridge with a little lemon juice added to retain colour.
5. Home-made juice will not last as long as a supermarket product because it contains no preservatives. **Drink it as soon as possible** to stop it discolouring and to retain vitamins and minerals.

▶

Choose a model with controls that are easy to operate with one hand – you will need the other to add the fruit and push the plunger.

Juice extractor features to look for

- **Centrifugal juicers:** use a circular filter basket with fine grating teeth to shred fruit/vegetables. When spun rapidly, centrifugal force separates juice from skin, pulp and pips. (Macerating juicers 'chew' the fruit and vegetables to remove juice – they give a thicker end product.)
- **Citrus press:** attachment that looks like a traditional lemon squeezer. Quicker than using a manual juicer to produce orange, lemon and lime juice. If you just want orange juice, choose a separate citrus press machine.
- **Juice-collecting jug:** separate jug for collecting extracted juice.
- **Juice spout:** directs juice straight into your glass.
- **Press on/off controls:** easier to use than dial controls.
- **Pulp collector:** compartment where all the skin, pulp and pips are collected.
- **Wide feed tube:** will cut down the amount of preparation fruit and vegetables will need.

Kitchenware

CHOPPING BOARDS

The larger the board, the more convenient to use. Choose one that can be used on both sides, keeping one side for strong-smelling foods. Buy colour-coded boards for foods such as raw meat and fish, to prevent cross-contamination.

For hygiene reasons, always use separate boards for preparing raw and cooked foods.

Marble and glass these boards can be rather unyielding and will blunt cutting blades very quickly. They are also very noisy to chop on. Marble and glass slabs are more suitable to use as a cool surface for pastry making.

Plastic Choose a polypropylene (PP) board – more expensive than polyethylene (HDPE) but more robust, more resistant to staining and less likely to crack under stress. Can also withstand higher washing temperatures so can be washed in dishwasher – the most hygienic cleaning method.

Wood Boards made from beech or other hardwoods such as maple, sycamore or rubberwood are most hardwearing. Ordinary wooden chopping boards are usually made in sections that are glued together for extra stability. End-grain chopping boards or blocks are expensive but are worth it because they are very hardwearing and robust.

 Clean wooden boards thoroughly and regularly.

KNIVES

Most professional knives need regular re-sharpening, so if you want a knife that stays sharp for years you may have to

5 TOP KNIFE-CARE TIPS

1. **Store knives separately**, either in a divided cutlery tray or a knife block. Magnetic knife racks should be placed well out of range of young children.
2. **Do not leave knives soaking** in the bottom of a washing-up bowl – it is easy to forget they are there.
3. **Dry knives immediately** after washing.
4. **Do not leave knives in the dishwasher** on a rinse-and-hold programme.
5. Use **separate knives** for preparing raw and cooked foods.

▶

compromise on quality of cutting. Most knives today are made of stainless steel, which is resistant to rusting. Reputable brands come with instructions for care and use – generally, knives with plastic handles are dishwasher-safe; most knives with wooden handles are not.

THE RIGHT KNIFE FOR THE JOB

TYPE OF KNIFE	USE
Bread knife	Serrated to slice bread without tearing.
Cook's knife (20–25cm/ 8–10in)	Versatile knife for chopping and slicing. The bigger it is, the more control you have over cutting.
Paring knife	For trimming, paring and decorating vegetables.
Serrated knife	For slicing fruit.

Knife features to look for

- **Evenly balanced weight between handle and blade:** check by resting knife across your fingers – it should remain level.
- **Full tang:** blade should continue inside handle to the end. Substantial handle with a good grip.

Sabatier knives

Do not assume that if a knife says Sabatier it will automatically be top quality. The name is used by several different French manufacturers who produce knives of similar design and styling. Judge a knife on its own merits.

PANS

Before buying new pans, check that they are suitable for use on your hob. This information is usually available in manufacturers' leaflets, or on the pan base.

SEE ALSO
Care and cleaning

Aluminium Available as non-stick coated, enamel coated (usually on exterior with a non-stick coating inside), hard-anodised (see below), or cast aluminium – which looks like cast iron but has the weight and good heat conductivity of aluminium. Uncoated aluminium pans are not suitable for cooking acidic foods.

Cast iron Heats up slowly but retains heat well, so good for long, even cooking at a low heat. Cast iron rusts easily on its own so pans usually have a non-stick interior coating or a thin protective layer of vitreous enamel. Uncoated cast iron is not dishwasher-safe. Very heavy; suitable for range cookers.

Copper Excellent heat conduction. Good copper pans are very expensive but should last a lifetime. As copper reacts with certain foods, pans are normally lined with tin or stainless steel to act as a barrier – unlined copper pans should be kept for display only. Copper pans have to be cleaned periodically with a proprietary copper polish.

IMPORTANT

Do not use copper pans on a glass-topped hob unless they have a sandwich-base construction.

Hard-anodised aluminium Distinguished by their steely grey or black colour. Surface has been electrochemically treated to produce a hard finish that will not chip, crack, peel or react with acidic foods. You can use metal utensils although these may leave marks on the surface of the pan. These pans are not usually dishwasher-safe but surface is stick-resistant – some pans have an additional non-stick coating. Hard-anodised pans are reasonably lightweight and heat up rapidly,

▶

CHOOSING PANS TO SUIT YOUR COOKER

HOB TYPE*	SUITABLE PANS
Ceramic hob	All pans except copper, stainless steel with exposed single-layer copper base, and glass ceramic. Make sure pan has a smooth, flat base to provide the best contact between hob and pan. A medium-weight pan is best. ■ Traditional cast-iron pans with rough bases can be used on a ceramic hob provided you are careful not to drag them across the glass. Some cast-iron pans have an enamel-coated base to reduce risk of scratching. Be careful not to drop pans on the hob. ■ Although copper pans are usually unsuitable for use on ceramic hobs, there are some copper-based pans suitable for glass-topped hobs due to their sandwich-base construction. ■ If you use glass pans on ceramic-glass hobs, cook on a medium to low heat otherwise the hob will get too hot and the thermal limiter may cut out more often, reducing cooking efficiency.
Electric radiant	All pans except copper, including stainless steel with an exposed single-layer copper base.
Gas	All pans. ■ Lightweight pans are better for gas as they will use the controllability of gas to its full potential. ■ Heavy-based pans such as cast iron will be slow to heat up, but because they retain their heat will allow you to cook at low temperatures.
Halogen	All pans except copper, stainless steel with exposed single-layer copper base and pans with reflective bases. Choose pans that have dull or dark bases – if the base is too bright and shiny the thermal limiter may cut out to prevent the glass overheating, so cooking will take longer.
Induction	The only suitable pans are ones made with a magnetic material in the base, such as cast iron or stainless steel.
Range cookers (eg Aga-Rayburn)	Check with cooker manufacturer. As a general guide, choose heavy-based pans, eg cast iron, to provide optimum contact with hob.
Sealed plate	All pans except copper, including stainless steel with exposed single-layer copper base.

* For an explanation of hob types, see pp.38–39.

eliminating hotspots. Expensive, but perform and last well.

Stainless steel Good quality pans should last a lifetime, but they can be expensive. Food tends to stick, so you use more oil. Stainless steel is a poor conductor of heat and is liable to have hot-spots, so different materials such as copper or aluminium are usually incorporated into the base to improve conductivity – these are sandwiched between two layers of stainless steel. Cooking on a low heat also helps. Stainless steel is dishwasher-safe and food does not react with it. Overheating and minerals in water may cause a 'rainbow effect' but a proprietary stainless-steel cleaner will remove these. Satin-finish pans mark less.

Pan coatings
- **Enamel:** usually applied to aluminium, cast-iron or steel pans. Price varies according to the metal underneath. Enamel pans will not pit, scratch easily or react with food. They can, however, chip if treated roughly. Heat distribution can be a problem with some pans – if coating is too thin, food may stick and burn, so avoid very lightweight pans, which can also warp over very high heat.
- **Non-stick:** ideal for frying, making sauces etc. A non-stick coating stops food sticking, reduces need for additional fat and is easy to clean. Non-stick coatings are applied to most types of cookware, from aluminium and steel to cast iron and stainless steel. Choose coating carefully as quality differs – look out for branded non-stick coatings such as Teflon or Silverstone that come with their own guarantee. Do not use metal utensils and abrasive scourers.

Pan features to look for
- **Dishwasher-safe:** as a general rule, pans with plastic or stainless steel handles or knobs are dishwasher-safe; most ▶

pans with wooden handles and knobs are not.

- **Flat base:** especially for electric cooking.
- **Oven-safe:** multi-purpose pans save time and storage space.
- **Pouring lips on both sides:** ideal for left-handers.
- **Size:** for energy-efficient cooking, buy pans similar in size to the hob ring.
- **Stay-cool and heatproof handles and knobs:** handles should be a good length and not too narrow.
- **Well-fitting lids:** but free enough to allow steam to escape if there are no steam vents.
- **Weight:** make sure pan will not be too heavy when full of food or water.

SEE ALSO

Dishwashers, p.43; microwave safe, p.98; China-matching services, Directory p.270

TABLEWARE

Before buying tableware, check that it is dishwasher-safe and suitable for use in your microwave.

Microwaves and combination ovens

A microwave will cook, reheat and defrost, but will not crisp or brown food. Combination ovens are more flexible and allow you to cook by microwave only, grill only or convection only; you can also use microwave and convection together (combination cooking) or microwave and grill together. Not all microwaves and combination ovens defrost well – some start to cook food. To defrost small amounts of food, use a low power level of around 180W for short bursts rather than the defrost setting.

When comparing models, the turntable size and interior height are more important than volume. For family use, turntable diameter should ideally be at least 30cm (12in) and

MATERIALS THAT CAN BE USED IN A MICROWAVE OVEN

China and ceramic	■ Only use if heat-resistant. If in doubt, do water test (see p.98). ■ Only use fine bone china for reheating for short periods – the change in temperature may crack dish or craze its finish. ■ Do not use dishes with a metallic trim.
Foil containers	Can be used if you follow certain guidelines: ■ Always check with manufacturer first. ■ Container must not touch any other metal such as a metal turntable or other container. ■ Take care container does not touch walls or door. ■ Food must not be totally encased in foil – there must be entry point for microwaves. ■ Food may take slightly longer to cook – check it is hot throughout before serving.
Heatproof glass (eg Pyrex)	A good choice. ■ Do not use delicate glass, which may crack with the heat from food.
Metal containers	Unsuitable for microwave-only ovens or microwaves with grills, but can be used in combination models when not in microwave-only mode – but check with manufacturer first.
Paper	Useful to prevent fatty foods spattering, and to stop foods like bread and pastries becoming soggy, but suitable for short cooking times only. Greaseproof and absorbent kitchen paper work well. ■ Do not use waxed and plastic-coated cups and plates as coating can melt into food.
Plastics	Most rigid plastics are suitable, but flexible ones tend not to be. ■ Do not use cream or margarine cartons or yogurt pots. ■ Avoid using plastics to cook foods with a high fat or sugar content as plastic may melt or distort. ■ Plastic freezer bags can be used for short periods of defrosting, but be careful of plastic ties containing metal wire.
Pottery, earthenware and stoneware	Only suitable if completely glazed.
Wicker and wood baskets	Can be used for quick heating of items such as bread rolls, but will dry out and crack if used too often or for too long. ■ Check basket does not contain metal staples. ■ Do not use wooden dishes.

Microwaves and combination ovens

interior height more than 20cm (8in) to accommodate larger portions of food. If thinking of buying a simple model with dial controls, check calibrations for first five minutes clearly show the all-important seconds.

Microwave features to look for

- **Auto cook/reheat/defrost:** automatically calculates power and length of cooking time.
- **Auto preheat:** maintains requested oven temperature for a set period, then automatically switches off.
- **Auto weight cook:** oven automatically calculates cooking time according to weight of food.
- **Delay start:** programmes oven to come on automatically at a later time.
- **One-touch controls:** for reheating specific foods – eg fish or milk – at the press of a button.
- **Quartz grill (bulbs set behind a metal mesh):** quick to heat and easy to clean. Less powerful than a conventional oven grill but more suitable for surface browning of food.
- **Radiant grill (as in a conventional oven):** better for cooking thicker foods, such as chops, but requires preheating and is less powerful than a conventional oven grill.
- **Stand timer:** can be set for a rest period during multi-stage cooking programme or at end of cooking, during which time food continues to cook from residual heat.

To test if your dishes are suitable for microwave cooking and reheating, fill a heat-resistant measuring jug with 300ml (11fl oz) cold water. Place on turntable alongside dish to be tested (if dish is large, stand jug on top of the empty dish) and heat on High for 1 minute. If dish is suitable it will remain cool while water in jug will begin to feel warm.

Music and television

DVD PLAYERS

Hold a whole movie in a package small enough to slip into your pocket, much harder to damage than a video tape, there's no tedious rewinding or fast-forwarding to find the beginning of a programme, and sound and picture quality are superb. Some programmes have interactive features – behind-the-scenes footage, several language soundtracks, and sports viewing from different angles, for example. DVD players also have built-in parental control – you can set a password to block access to programmes with an adult content. For DVD convenience and TV-quality sound, a basic model will do the job, but if you want the cinema experience at home, more expensive players add digital decoders that allow existing home cinema amplifiers to handle digital surround sound.

DVD features to look for

- **CD-R replay:** plays back audio CDs recorded on computer.
- **Chapters:** subdivision within a title (a DVD containing four episodes of a TV series would have four titles) that splits up programme or movie (title) to make it easy to jump to a particular point. Many DVDs also have a chapter selection screen that shows snapshots of the start of each chapter.
- **Coaxial output:** refers to the best way to send digital surround sound to a TV or amplifier that can play it.
- **Digital decoder:** enables player to be connected to a home cinema amplifier that cannot handle Dolby Digital or DTS signals. Gives the amp digital quality surround sound.
- **Dolby Digital (DD):** special soundtrack with up to six tracks of top-quality sound. This usually requires a digital decoder in your TV or amplifier.

▶

- **Dolby Pro Logic:** a surround-sound system – now largely superseded – that works through a SCART plug on TVs and amplifiers that support it.
- **Double layer:** means DVD has two sets of information on the same side, giving twice as much space. There's a short interval while player changes layers.
- **DTS:** rival of Dolby Digital that gives better results, according to manufacturers.
- **Optical output:** alternative way to send digital surround sound to a TV or amplifier capable of playing it.
- **Regions:** DVD divides the world into six regions (Europe is Region 2). Most DVDs are compatible only with players set up for the same region.
- **SCART plugs:** shaped like a stretched letter D with a kink at one end, commonly used to link a player to your TV.

SEE ALSO
Televisions, p.102

STEREO SYSTEMS

Think about how much you want to spend and how important sound quality is to you.

Compact systems Also known as mini or micro, but size is not a guide to quality or power, although larger speakers can give a fuller base sound. Systems vary considerably in price, but you get what you pay for – very cheap systems have low power and sound little better than a large portable.

SEE ALSO
British Audio Dealers' Association, Directory p.273

Hi-fi separates Much more expensive than compact systems. For music-lovers prepared to spend time in shop demonstration rooms doing some serious listening – but take your own CDs along. The separates route means you do not have to spend money on features you do not want. Specialist hi-fi dealers sell a much bigger range of separates than high street chains and superstores. The British Audio Dealers'

Association can supply a list.

Stereo features to look for

- **Auto reverse:** when one side of a cassette finishes the next side starts playing.
- **CD-R/RW:** allows you to play recordable and re-recordable CDs created on your computer.
- **DAB (Digital Audio Broadcasting):** digital signals produce a much clearer sound.
- **DIN, EIAS, MPO or RMS:** power output measuring systems that are not comparable with each other. Output is often given as so many DIN or whatever 'per channel', indicating how much power comes out of each speaker.
- **Magnetic shielding:** lets you place hi-fi speakers near TVs or other large electrical appliances without interference.
- **Mini discs:** a digital alternative to tapes; you can rearrange order of tracks and record over them hundreds of times.
- **Optical input:** radio signal comes in the form of light rather than through standard wires, so this should enable you to get a better signal.
- **Pre-set stations:** you can save positions of your favourite radio stations instead of having to find them every time.
- **Programmable CD player:** lets you choose the order you want tracks to be played in.
- **RDS (Radio Data System):** searches for strongest signal and displays name of station the radio is tuned to.
- **RF remote:** remote control that works even if you are in another room (as opposed to an infra red remote, which has to be pointed at the appliance for it to work).

TELEVISIONS

The three main choices are of screen size and format, sound capabilities and whether the TV is digital. Most sets are 70cm ▶

(28in) or 80cm (32in) (the diagonal measurement of the screen) – a 70cm (28in) screen, for example, is around 60cm (24in) wide and 32cm (13in) high. Widescreen sets are almost twice as wide as they are high, and very heavy – a 70cm (28in) set typically weighs 40kg (88lb). Most new sets have Nicam stereo, the standard for TV broadcasts, but some add surround sound – this means having small speakers behind the viewer, which involves wires trailing around the room.

Widescreen TVs There are two good reasons for going widescreen. First, it is more natural as our eyes supply us with a widescreen view of the world. Second, it is the way TV broadcasting is going – most new programmes are made in widescreen. When the picture is sent out on a standard screen, it either has the edges cut off, losing some of the action, or there are black bars at the top and bottom of the screen. On a digital TV service, the full image is available if you have a widescreen TV.

Plasma screens TVs so thin they can be hung on the wall. Extremely expensive but have huge screens – the most common is 170cm (42in) – and produce excellent results.

Combi TVs The combined 34cm (14in) TV set and video recorder – known as a combi TV, TVCR or televideo – is ideal for a second set. It doesn't need a TV stand and won't dominate a small room, and some combi TVs have a built-in child lock or security lock. However, the cheapest are simply basic video recorders with a screen attached – fine for watching TV or a video but you cannot record one channel while watching another. Another drawback is that most set fronts feature only the basic channel, volume and

VCR controls, so if you lose your remote control you will lose access to the brightness, contrast and colour balance as well as channel tuning.

TV features to look for

- **Dolby ProLogic:** surround-sound system designed to reproduce cinema-type sound in the home.
- **Fastext:** lets you move between Teletext pages using the four coloured buttons on remote control.
- **Flicker-reduced picture:** picture is put on screen 100 times a second (100Hz) instead of the usual 50Hz, improving picture quality on large screens (60cm/24in plus).
- **Integrated digital decoder:** allows you to watch free-to-view digital channels without buying a separate set-top box. Look for a DVB sticker on the screen, which means the same thing.
- **Multi TV system reception:** useful if you plan to take a TV abroad because it allows you to pick up the signal of other countries that use different broadcasting systems.
- **NICAM:** the stereo sound system found on most new TVs.
- **NTSC playback:** lets you watch video cassettes recorded in US or Japanese format.
- **Optical input:** TV signal comes in the form of light rather than through wires, which should mean you receive better and cleaner pictures.
- **PIP:** stands for picture in picture; you can see one programme in miniature in corner of screen while watching a different one on rest of screen.
- **SCART sockets:** allow you to plug other equipment such as a DVD or video player or a satellite box in to your TV. Think about how many you're going to need before you buy.
- **16:9:** the width by depth ratio of a widescreen TV (a 'normal' TV is 4:3, four units wide to three units high).

▶

Safety equipment

SMOKE ALARMS

Essential protection in any home – and any smoke alarm is better than no smoke alarm. Install at least one on each floor. One of the newest styles – the Fire Angel Smoke Alarm, available at B&Q and other DIY stores – is simply plugged into a pendant bayonet-bulb light fitting before inserting the bulb. Because its built-in battery automatically recharges when the light is switched on, it is unaffected by power cuts.

Steam cleaners

These work like an oversized kettle, using tap water to create steam and clean surfaces without detergents. They claim to shift grime from everything – ovens, carpets, ceramic tiles, windows – you can even use one to defrost the freezer. But, in most cases, conventional methods give better results and are easier and quicker. Manufacturers point out that steam cleaners are not designed to deep-clean carpets and that they are more suitable for refreshing and lifting pile. If you are considering buying a steam cleaner because you are sensitive to certain household detergents or have asthma, contact Allergy UK for advice.

Toasters

Toasters now offer a host of options from one-side and sandwich toasting to roll and croissant warming. Look for

Music and television

safety features – but avoid leaving the room while the toaster is in use.

WARNING

Never poke a knife in to remove an item – unplug the toaster and use a plastic spatula.

Toaster features to look for

- **Cancel option:** lets you turn off toaster mid-cycle.
- **Cool walls:** keep outside of toaster cool enough to touch.
- **Extra lift:** pushes small slices and teacakes above slots for safe removal.
- **Frozen bread setting:** defrosts and toasts bread straight from freezer.
- **One-side toasting:** for teacakes and buns that need toasting on one side only.
- **Reheat facility:** warms toast that has cooled down without over-browning.
- **Removable crumb rack:** for a mess-free worktop.
- **Safety cut-out:** in case pop-up does not work, or if bread jams in toaster.
- **Single slice setting:** saves energy when you want to toast just one slice.
- **Variable width slots:** accommodate everything from thin slices to doorsteps – useful for muffins and bagels.
- **Warming rack:** lets you heat items like rolls and croissants – can be integral or detachable.

Vacuum cleaners

Traditionally, cylinder vacuum cleaners relied mostly on suction, while uprights had a rotating brush in the cleaning head, called a beater bar. These days, the distinction between the two is not so clear-cut – some cylinders now have a turbo brush attachment that mirrors the action of a beater bar, improving their performance at picking up pet hairs and raising carpet pile, while some uprights now allow you to switch off beater bar (which can cause damage to polished wood floors, tiles and loop-pile carpets) so they function more like a cylinder.

CYLINDER CLEANERS

- Generally have a small and compact body, making them light to carry around – a real plus if you have lots of stairs, suffer from arthritis or have back problems.
- Are better at cleaning edges than uprights, and are easier to use in furniture-filled rooms.
- Can be stored in a small place.
- Usually have smaller dust bags than an upright, so bags fill up more quickly and will need changing frequently.

UPRIGHT CLEANERS

- Have a raised floor head that glides along on wheels, so less

UPRIGHT OR CYLINDER?	
FLOOR TYPE	YOUR CHOICE OF CLEANER
Cut-pile carpet	■ Upright ■ Cylinder with turbo brush attachment
Loop-pile carpet	■ Cylinder
Natural floor covering (eg seagrass, coir) Ceramic tiles, stone, wood, lino or vinyl	■ Upright with beater bar that can be switched off
Mixture of all the above floor coverings	■ Upright with beater bar that can be switched off ■ Cylinder with turbo brush attachment

effort is required to push.

- Are more cumbersome, but some people find the upright position more comfortable.
- Tend to be less effective than cylinders at cleaning edges; however, most come with a set of tools to enable you to get into awkward corners.

3-in-1 cleaners These wash carpets and upholstery, sucking the moisture out as part of the process, as well as vacuuming.

Special requirements

SEE ALSO

Allergy UK, Directory
p.273

- If you have pets: a cleaner with a beater bar or turbo brush will help lift pet hairs, but do not use beater bars or turbo brushes on loop-pile or natural floor coverings.
- If you suffer from allergies or asthma: look for a vacuum cleaner with a filter efficiency of at least 95 per cent. Filter efficiency refers to the amount of tiny dust particles the cleaner retains, not to its pick-up performance. Empty a bagless vacuum cleaner outside and tip it straight into a plastic bin liner. Allergy UK can supply details of vacuum cleaners that have The British Allergy Foundation Seal of Approval.

PART 2

Care and cleaning

THE GOOD HOUSEKEEPING INSTITUTE regularly
tests cleaning and stain removal remedies in response
to a vast number of queries. Part 2 contains the Institute's
findings and includes hundreds of tried and tested cleaning
tips – the most important one being to follow any
manufacturers' recommendations. Products mentioned are
available from supermarkets, department stores, hardware
stores and specialist shops, or by mail order.

Household surfaces

IN THIS CHAPTER YOU WILL FIND

Here's how to clean and maintain household surfaces, the best time- and labour-saving tips and where to go for professional advice.

Bathroom fittings

SEE ALSO

Taps, p.113

BATHS

Acrylic Rinse bath after use to prevent water staining. Clean regularly with an all-purpose bathroom cleaner to prevent build-up of dirt and scum. For stubborn marks, use a nylon bristle brush but not an abrasive cleaner. In hard water areas, use a limescale cleaner; check label before use. Pay special attention to area around taps.

■ **Scratches:** rub fine scratches gently with metal polish, then clean the bath.

Vitreous enamel-coated cast iron or steel Clean as for acrylic baths, but use only products recommended by the Vitreous Enamel Association, and a soft cloth. Products with anti-limescale ingredients, may cause enamel to dull. Remove limescale with a solution of half vinegar and half water, applied with a soft cloth to the area of limescale – avoid getting vinegar on other parts of the enamel. Rinse thoroughly and dry. Alternatively, try using a plastic scourer, neat washing-up liquid and lots of elbow grease.

■ **If your bath is old:** it may not be able to take modern cleaners, so test all products on a small area first.

▶

■ **Bath resurfacing:** if your enamel bath has become matt, or damaged by scale deposits and abrasives, you can have the surface professionally cleaned and polished. However, if damage is severe, you may need to have it resurfaced – though it may be more economical to buy a new bath. Companies that offer resurfacing include Bathroom Renovations Ltd, Interbaths Resurfacing Services, and Renubath Services Ltd.

Whirlpool and spa baths Although most are self-draining, it is important to clean out scum left in pipework. Once a week, fill bath with water and add a cleaning agent (the manufacturer's proprietary product or a cupful of mild sterilising liquid, such as Milton). Allow to circulate for five minutes. Empty bath, refill with clean water and circulate for a further five minutes to rinse.

BASINS
Clean with an all-purpose bathroom cleaner and wipe with a damp cloth. Make sure plug-hole is rinsed thoroughly as bathroom cleaners can damage the coating. Buff brass or gold-plated plug-holes after use to prevent discolouration.

SEALANT
To remove mould, use a fungicidal spray, such as Dettox Mould and Mildew Bathroom Cleaner, and spray regularly to prevent regrowth. Once sealant has gone black, mould is impossible to remove.

SHOWERS
■ **Shower tray:** clean with an all-purpose bathroom cleaner. If in a hard-water area, use a limescale remover once a week.
■ **Shower screens:** clean with a solution of washing-up liquid.

SEE ALSO
Mildew, p.200; Plastic shower curtains, p.201

On folding shower screens pay particular attention to the hinging mechanism, which can get grubby. Use a limescale remover to remove white watermarks.

- **Shower heads:** descale using a liquid descaler and an old toothbrush. Alternatively, steep it in a solution of half distilled vinegar, half water and leave for a couple of hours.
- **Mould:** damp areas are susceptible to mould, which appears as black spores. To remove, spray with fungicide and re-spray regularly to prevent further growth.
- **Grout:** if grout between tiles becomes dirty and discoloured, apply a whitening product that contains a fungicide. Alternatively, clean with an old toothbrush and a solution of diluted household bleach (one part bleach to four parts water), although this does not contain mould inhibitors.

TAPS

SEE ALSO
Baths, p.111

Products such as toothpaste can damage protective coating on taps, particularly those with a gold or brass finish. Ideally, wipe taps and buff dry after every use. Clean regularly with a solution of washing-up liquid, rinse and dry. Do not use an abrasive cleaner. To remove heavy limescale deposits, soak a cloth in a proprietary descaler and wrap around tap. Do not leave for longer than the recommended time. Rinse thoroughly and dry.

TOILETS

SEE ALSO
Dripping overflow, p.224

Wipe all seats, including wooden ones, with a solution of washing-up liquid. To keep bowl clean, use a bathroom cleaner with added disinfectant, or fit an in-cistern cleaner or bowl cleaner to release cleaner or bleach with every flush. Clean the outside of the bowl and the cistern with a solution of washing-up liquid or a bathroom cleaner. For thorough cleaning of bowl, use a liquid or powder cleaner and a toilet ▶

brush, paying particular attention to under the rim, or a mousse that expands under the rim. Keep brush clean by rinsing in bleach after use.

- **Limescale:** in hard water areas, use a toilet cleaner with built-in limescale remover. To remove limescale in the bowl, use a limescale remover with a thick gel consistency. For heavy deposits, empty water from bowl first – bail out by hand or, if cistern is accessible, tie up the float-operated inlet valve (ballcock) and flush the toilet.

WARNING

Do not use two different toilet cleaners at the same time. When they mix, toxic gases can be released.

Blinds (wood and metal)

SEE ALSO

Austrian/Festoon Blinds, p.176; Roller Blinds, p.176

BAMBOO
Wipe clean with a solution of washing-up liquid, then dry with a cloth.

VENETIAN
Use a special dusting brush, available from hardware stores. Alternatively, wearing cotton gloves, run your hands along both sides of the slats. A vacuum cleaner upholstery attachment can also be used.

Chandeliers

Always turn off the electricity before starting to clean.

- **Occasional cleaning:** use a dedicated cleaner, such as Antiquax Crystal and Chandelier Cleaner. Clean in situ by spraying on and allowing cleaner to run off along with dirt. Protect floor with polythene, old towels and newspaper.
- **Thorough cleaning:** turn off the electricity before starting to

clean. Remove as much of the chandelier as possible from the light fitting. Wash using a warm solution of washing-up liquid, then pat dry with a lint-free cloth.

Chopping boards

LAMINATED MELAMINE

These boards, which usually have a picture on one side, are not dishwasher-proof and should never be soaked. Wipe over with a solution of washing-up liquid and dry immediately.

PLASTIC

Clean in hot, soapy water and dry thoroughly. If stained, soak overnight in a mild solution of bleach, then wash in hot, soapy water. Some plastic chopping boards can be washed in the dishwasher, which is the most hygienic method.

WOOD

Rinse the board under very hot water. Never soak as the wood will swell, and crack on drying. Leave to dry naturally, resting on one edge. Do not dry flat, which could cause warping and also speed up the multiplication of bacteria. Once in a while, wipe over with an anti-bacterial product.

IMPORTANT

Always replace a cracked, severely scored or stained board, whatever material it is made from.

Cookers

COOKER HOODS

Clean filters regularly – some hoods have indicator lights that tell you when filters need cleaning or replacing. Charcoal and paper filters are not washable and should be replaced regularly ▶

– charcoal every three to four months, paper every two months. Metal filters can be cleaned in a hot solution of washing-up liquid, soaking for a few hours if really greasy. Some metal filters can be washed in a dishwasher.

For maximum efficiency, and to stop smells lingering after cooking, switch on hood 10-15 minutes before you start cooking and run it for a few minutes afterwards. Some hoods automatically switch off after a set time.

HOBS

Gas Some pan supports and spillage wells are dishwasher-safe. Otherwise use a suitable cream cleaner and a damp cloth. If possible, remove control knobs as dirt can build up behind them. Clean metal surround with a proprietary metal cleaner.

Metal cleaners, p.128

Glass-topped (including all ceramic, halogen and induction hobs) Turn off hob and make sure surface is cool before cleaning. A paper towel or clean damp cloth should remove light soiling, or use a specialist hob cleaner. Stubborn stains and cooked-on food deposits should be removed using the special hob scraper provided with the hob (or available from hardware stores), which will not damage glass. After cleaning, use a proprietary hob conditioner such as Hob Brite to protect glass.

- **Sugar-based spills:** turn off heat immediately, remove pan and very carefully wipe glass before continuing cooking. If you leave sugar, it will crystallise on cooling and cause pitting.
- **To avoid scratches:** always lift pans when moving them across the hob. Check base of pan is clean and dry.

Sealed plates Make sure plates are turned off. Clean using a scourer and cream cleaner, rubbing in a circular pattern following the grooves on the hob plates. To avoid rusting and maintain colour, apply a proprietary hob conditioner such as Hob Brite after cleaning. Wear rubber gloves, and use a strong cloth as the steel plates have a rough texture. On re-heating, plates will smoke slightly and will smell – this is normal.

SEE ALSO

Microwaves and combination ovens, p.148; Oven Cleaning Systems, p.42

OVENS

Most modern cookers have stay-clean oven linings. Never attempt to clean these. To clean ordinary enamel linings and oven floor, use a proprietary cleaner such as Mr Muscle Oven Cleaner, making sure it does not come into contact with stay-clean linings. Always wear rubber gloves and make sure that the room is well ventilated.

- **To make cleaning easier:** place a bowl of water in the oven and heat on a high temperature for 20 minutes, to help loosen dirt and grease. Wipe away any condensation with cloth or a paper towel.
- **Kitchen tiles:** to remove burnt-on grease splashes behind your hob, use a solution of sugar soap, available from DIY stores. Wear rubber gloves and apply with a cloth.

TIP

After cleaning, use a cloth to smear a thin paste of bicarbonate of soda and water on enamel linings. This dries to leave a protective layer that absorbs greasy soiling and makes it easier to clean next time.

OVEN DOORS

Remove cooked-on deposits with a metal spatula or ceramic hob scraper, then use a spray-on oven cleaner. If glass in door is removable, soak in a solution of biological washing powder.

OVEN SHELVES

Clean in the dishwasher if possible. Remove racks before drying cycle and chip off residue with the back of a knife. Alternatively, soak shelves in a hot biological washing detergent solution in the bath if the sink isn't big enough. Any remaining deposits can be removed with a mild abrasive cleaner or soap-impregnated pad. If you wish to use an oven cleaner, check first that it is suitable on chrome.

Doors

SEE ALSO

Metals, p.128

DOOR FURNITURE

Clean hinges, handles and locks according to the metal they're made from and any special finish.

PVCU (ALSO KNOWN AS UPVC)

Remove dirt using a proprietary PVCu frame and furniture cleaner, such as Nilco uPVC Cleaner or HG Plastic Furniture Cleaner to prevent permanent yellowing.

WOOD

Wipe wood or painted wood with a damp cloth and solution of washing-up liquid. Use a neat washing-up liquid on stains and rub along grain with a soft cloth. Avoid over-wetting.

Driveways and patios

Remove build-up of grime and algae with a high-pressure washer, which blasts off the algae with a jet of water. However, these can remove pointing between paving stones if you are not careful. If you do not have an outdoor electricity supply or a garden hose connected to a tap, try scrubbing with a stiff brush and specialist patio cleaner. Household bleach is a cheap, quick alternative. For heavy staining use an acid-based cleaner. Products containing a fungicide will help inhibit future regrowth of algae.

 IMPORTANT Take care when applying cleaning products near plants or grass, or in areas that are used by children or pets.

Fireplaces

 SEE ALSO

Tiles, p.121; Marble, p.124

Where possible, refer to manufacturer's cleaning instructions. Wear goggles to protect yourself from flaking particles.

CAST AND WROUGHT IRON

Remove any surface dust by wiping with a dry cloth or using the brush attachment on your vacuum cleaner. Remove any rust on grate and surround with a wire brush or wire wool, or treat with a proprietary rust remover such as Liberon Rust Remover or Hammerite Rust Remover Gel. Re-blacken iron using Liberon Iron Paste or Zebo Black Grate Polish – work in sections, applying a small amount with a cloth, then buffing to a shine with a brush. Alternatively, apply a heat-resistant aerosol paint, such as barbecue paint, Woodstove from Plasti-Kote or Hammerite's Decorative High Heat Paint (both available from DIY stores), for a long-term finish.

 IMPORTANT Do not use water to clean uncoated iron, as this will encourage rust to form.

Flooring (hard)

Vacuum or sweep hard floors regularly to avoid surface scratching by grit. If possible, follow manufacturers' recommendations for sealants and polishes.

▶

SEE ALSO

Care and cleaning,
carpets, pp.177–178

CORK

Wipe clean factory-sealed cork tiles with a damp mop, using a solution of washing-up liquid. To give an extra protective layer, especially in areas such as the kitchen or bathroom, apply an acrylic or polyurethane sealant.

IMPORTANT

Never over-wet, and take care not to damage seal or protective coating by dragging appliances or furniture over it.

LAMINATE

Vacuum, dust or wipe with a damp mop or cloth – never use soap-based detergents or other polishes, as they may leave a dull film on the floor, and avoid over-wetting. Do not use wax polish. To remove marks and stains, use a dilute solution of vinegar and water – never be tempted to use abrasive cleaners, including nylon scouring pads and steel wool, which can scratch the floor. Stubborn marks such as shoe polish can be removed with nail polish remover containing acetone or other mild alcohol-based solvents.

TIP

To protect a laminate floor, put felt pads underneath furniture legs, and drip trays under planted pots.

LINOLEUM

Sweep or vacuum surface to remove grit and dust. Clean with a mop or cloth dampened with a solution of detergent or floor cleaner. Use water sparingly. Rinse after washing.
- **Stubborn marks:** rub lightly with a fine nylon pad, available from supermarkets, and neat detergent.
- **Polishing:** if you prefer a glossy finish, use an emulsion water-based polish twice a year. Apply one thin coat at a time and allow to dry completely before applying another one. Do not use wax polish.

SEE ALSO

Care and cleaning,
carpets, pp.177–178

MATTING

Coir Vacuum regularly with a suction-only-type cylinder cleaner to keep it dust-free. Treat stains immediately – you should be able to mop up spills with absorbent paper or a sponge, then wipe over with clean warm water.

Rush Vacuum as regularly as carpet, lifting occasionally to vacuum underneath. Treat stains with a solution of warm water and washing soda. Occasionally scrub over matting with soap and warm water.

Seagrass Vacuum regularly. Sponge up any spills.

Sisal Check manufacturer's instructions and use cleaning products such as Crucial Trading Care and Cleaning Box.

STONE (INCLUDING SLATE, FLAGSTONES, GRANITE AND MARBLE)

Stone should be protected with a resin sealant as it is susceptible to staining. To clean sealed stone, first vacuum thoroughly, then mop with a mild detergent solution. To remove grease or oil, use a proprietary spot stain remover such as HG Worldpoint Spot Stain Remover.

TILES

Ceramic Tiles need minimal maintenance – sweep and wash with a mild detergent solution. Rinse with clear water. Do not polish. Tile cleaning products are available at tile outlets.
- **Grouting:** clean dirty grout with a soft brush dipped in a mild solution of bleach, then rinse well. Specialist grout-cleaning products can be bought from tile outlets.

▶

Quarry Simply sweep and wash with a neutral detergent. Rinse with clear water. Do not polish. Specialist tile cleaning produc are available from tile outlets.

Quarry tiles do not need any sealant or polish. To restore fadec colour, use specialist cleaning products to remove polish.

Terracotta For the first year after installation, terracotta tiles mature. Most suppliers stock specialist cleaner, sealant and polish so make enquiries at the point of sale and use recommended products. Older floors may have traces of linsee oil on them, so in 'wet' areas such as kitchens, bathrooms and utility rooms, use a specialist floor sealant that will not react with it, such as Liberon Floor Sealer. In 'dry' areas, if you prefe a wax finish, apply a floor wax by Liberon or Fila. New floors are more absorbent, so to protect tiles from staining and water damage, apply several coats of sealant materials.

VINYL

Sweep with a soft brush or vacuum, then wipe over with a dan cloth or sponge, using a solution of detergent or floor cleaner. Rinse thoroughly after wiping.

- **To remove scuff marks:** use a cloth dipped in neat washing-up liquid or white spirit, then rinse off.
- **For extra hygiene:** if you have pets and/or young children you may want to add a little disinfectant to the detergent solution

WOOD

Sealed Sealed floors only need to be swept and damp-mopped. Do not use too much water as wood swells. If you wish, apply an emulsion polish on top of the varnish, but remove after several applications using a proprietary wax remover such as

Rustins Surface Cleaner or a floor cleaner to which you have added a little ammonia (which is available from chemists or hardware stores).

IMPORTANT Do not apply a wax – even a non-slip wax will make a wooden floor very slippery and dangerous to walk on.

Unsealed and waxed Sweep regularly and occasionally apply wax polish – but use sparingly as too much wax will leave a tacky surface and attract dirt. Buff well. If worn patches appear in the surface, apply a non-slip floor polish. On waxed floors, polish and dirt builds up over time and the only way to clean them is to remove the wax and start again. Use a cloth moistened with white spirit. Let it soak in, and as the wax and dirt begin to dissolve, wipe away with crumpled newspaper. Scrub obstinate parts by hand, or with abrasive pads on a floor polisher. When polish has been removed, damp-mop with clean water. Allow to dry completely before applying new polish, working over small sections at a time.

IMPORTANT Do not varnish a waxed floor as it will not dry.

Furniture

SEE ALSO

Leather, p.160;
Problem Solving,
marks on furniture,
pp.221–223

FRENCH POLISHED

Dust regularly with a soft cloth. Remove sticky marks with a cloth wrung out in a warm, mild solution of soapflakes, taking care not to over-wet. Dry thoroughly with a soft cloth. Use a wax polish occasionally and sparingly.

■ **Professional restoration:** serious damage on valuable pieces should be repaired professionally. Contact the British Antique Furniture Restorers' Association for recommendations.

▶

Heat-resistant mats to put under tablecloths: John Lewis, Wilds Table Felts, Directory pp.271 and 272

LACQUERED WOOD

Wipe with a damp duster. Apply a fine water-mist spray directly on to the duster to avoid over-wetting the wood. Wipe dry and buff with a soft, dry duster. Occasionally apply a good furniture polish to revive shine.

- **Grease:** remove grease and finger-marks with a damp cloth and a mild solution of soapflakes. Take care not to over-wet. Dry thoroughly with a soft cloth.

LLOYD LOOM

Vacuum with a nozzle attachment. A small, stiff brush may help loosen dust. Wash down using a solution of washing-up liquid and a soft brush. Do not over-wet. Rinse and allow to dry out thoroughly.

MARBLE

Wipe over with a solution of washing-up liquid. Polish once or twice a year with a proprietary marble polish such as HG Worldpoint Marble Stain Remover or Bell Special Marble Cleaner, to bring back shine.

- **Stains:** treat with turpentine – this may take several attempts. If any stain remains, cut a lemon in half and rub on affected area – but only allow the lemon to remain in contact with the marble for a few moments, and rinse away all traces afterwards. Alternatively, try a proprietary cleaner such as Lithofin Oil-Ex and follow treatment with Lithofin Stain-Stop to protect marble from future accidents.

TO REMOVE SMELLS FROM WARDROBE INTERIORS
Try an air freshener such as Neutradol Original Gel, which absorbs smells rather than just masking them with fragrance. Place the pot on one of the shelves and keep cupboard door closed as much as possible.

■ **Chips and marks:** to deal with severe chipping and marking, call in a professional: contact the Stone Federation.

WAXED WOOD
Dust regularly with a soft cloth. Remove sticky marks with a cloth wrung out in a warm, mild solution of soapflakes, taking care not to over-wet. Dry thoroughly with a soft cloth.
■ **Polishing:** apply a wax polish once or twice a year. Solid wax produces the best results but requires lots of elbow grease.

Garden furniture

SEE ALSO

Canvas, p.155

CANE
Retain the manufacturer's cleaning instructions for reference. Most items only need vacuuming with an upholstery nozzle, or a wipe with a damp cloth to remove dust. Never leave cane furniture outdoors.

CAST ALUMINIUM
Wipe clean with a solution of washing-up liquid. Touch up chipped paint with enamel metal paint after rubbing off any loose paint with wire wool. The manufacturer may supply a touch-up kit.

CAST AND WROUGHT IRON
Wearing protective goggles, rub down with wire wool and repaint with anti-rust primer and exterior metal paint. Use a wire brush or rust-removing paint to shift flaking rust. Repaint as above.

SYNTHETIC RESIN
Use a detergent solution and a plastic brush to clean. Remove stains with a mild solution of household bleach. Rinse well. ▶

TUBULAR METAL

Wash down plastic-coated furniture with a warm solution of washing-up liquid. Protect with a light application of wax polish. Store indoors.

WOOD

- **Durable:** woods such as teak, iroko, western red cedar, American mahogany, pitch pine or oak do not usually need preserving. Wipe over with teak oil twice a year to help preserve colour.
- **Non-durable:** woods such as ash, beech, elm, European redwood, pine and spruce need preserving. Apply a proprietary wood preservative such as Cuprinol, followed by a good varnish.
- **Painted and varnished:** rub down with fine sandpaper, then reapply coating using an appropriate wood finish.

Grouting

See Ceramic tiles, p.134.

Gutters

SEE ALSO

Drains/Blockages, p.220

Prevent blockages by checking and cleaning gutters annually, before winter sets in. Clip netting over guttering to prevent leaves or birds' nests accumulating – check this too, as anything that collects in the netting may make it sag into the gutter, causing a blockage. Cast iron guttering needs regular cleaning and painting to prevent rust.

Kitchen units

SEE ALSO
Work surfaces, p.134

DOORS

- **Coloured/wood effect:** wipe with a damp cloth and washing-up liquid solution, taking care not to over-wet surface. Rub stains carefully with a slightly abrasive cream cleaner.
- **High-gloss surfaces:** these can easily be scratched, so use a soft cloth and make sure it is free from grit. Wipe thoroughly with a dry cloth. Use neat washing-up liquid on stains, rubbing gently with a soft cloth.
- **Wood/wood veneer:** wipe with a damp cloth and washing-up liquid solution. Use a neat solution of washing-up liquid on stains, rubbing along grain with a soft cloth.

INTERIORS

Remove all items and wipe surfaces with a damp cloth and antibacterial cleaner or washing-up liquid solution. Replace items when thoroughly dry. Take care not to soak exposed chipboard and around hinge joints where water can seep through to chipboard.

Lampshades

SEE ALSO
Fabric lampshades,
p.180

GLASS/PLASTIC

Dust regularly or use a clean cloth and a solution of washing-up liquid.

PAPER/PARCHMENT

Brush often with a feather duster. Avoid wetting.

RAFFIA/STRAW

Vacuum using the dusting brush attachment.

▶

Metals

COPPER AND BRASS

Wash in a warm solution of washing-up liquid, brush gently with a soft brush, rinse and dry with a soft cloth. Then use one of the following polishing methods:

- **Creams/liquids:** these are usually applied with a cloth and buffed before polish has completely dried. Some polishes can be rinsed off with water and are ideal for intricate pieces.
- **Wadding:** for heavier tarnishing, use copper or brass wadding impregnated with polish. This is messy and requires elbow grease. Do not use too frequently as it is quite abrasive.
- **DIY method:** if you only have one or two small pieces to clean and don't want to buy a proprietary cleaner, try rubbing the surface with half a lemon dipped in salt. Rinse and buff dry with a soft cloth. This method, however, tends to lighten copper and bring out the orange colour.

Verdigris for heavy, green corrosion use proprietary rust remover such as Rustins Rust Remover. Apply with a paintbrush and gently rub surface with fine steel wool. Clean with metal polish.

LACQUERED ITEMS

These only need dusting and occasional washing in warm, soapy water. If lacquer wears away, remove with a proprietary paint remover, then polish brass or copper as above. Reapply transparent lacquer such as Rustins Clear Metal Lacquer or have the item professionally lacquered.

■ **If you live by the sea:** You can buy PVD door furniture that is specially treated to cope with environmental factors such as sea spray, and comes with a 25-year guarantee. Stockists include Samuel Heath, Bernards and M Brock Ltd.

PEWTER

About once a year, wash in warm, soapy water and dry well with a soft cloth. Never use harsh polish. If pewter is heavily tarnished, use a proprietary silver cleaner such as Silvo.

■ **Antique items:** for details of professional cleaners of antique pewter, contact the Association of British Pewter Craftsmen.

SILVER

Wash promptly after use, using a warm solution of washing-up liquid and a soft cloth. Rinse in hot water and dry. When dusting, use impregnated silver polishing cloths and mitts – but remember that silver is a soft metal, so do not rub too hard as you could scratch the surface. Use straight, even strokes – never rub silver crosswise or with a rotary movement. Use one of these methods to polish silverware:

■ **Creams/liquids:** often recommended by manufacturers of fine silver services, these are ideal to clean medium tarnishing. Allow to dry to a fine, powdery deposit, then buff with a dry cloth. Some require rinsing in water, so are ideal for cutlery that needs to be washed after cleaning anyway.

■ **Foaming silver pastes:** ideal for cutlery, and for covering larger areas such as platters, these are easy to use. The paste is applied with a damp sponge and lathers to a foam. Rinse in water and dry thoroughly.

■ **Sprays:** good for covering larger areas.

■ **Wadding:** for heavier tarnishing. This is messy and requires elbow grease. Do not use too frequently as it is quite abrasive.

▶

■ **Dips:** not recommended by experts as they leave silver duller with less lustre. Best for small items such as jewellery – though do not use on pearls, coral or opals. Only suitable for light tarnish. Always follow manufacturer's time limits. Do not use dips on heavily tarnished items – they can produce a dull white finish. Avoid getting dip on stainless steel knife blades as it can stain or etch the surface.

■ **DIY dip:** line a plastic washing-up bowl with aluminium foil. Fill with very hot water and add a handful of washing soda. Immerse tarnished silver, ensuring it is in contact with foil. For large items that come above the water line, turn after five minutes. Do not immerse items for more than 10 minutes. Replace foil when it darkens.

For specific silver items, try the following:

■ **Silver teapots:** remove tarnishing, water scale and tea stains using a silver dip such as Goddards Silver Dip. Pour the contents of the dip into teapot and swirl around. Rinse well before using.

■ **Lacquered items:** as lacquered copper and brass (see p.128).

■ **Cutlery:** never mix silver and stainless steel cutlery in a dishwasher as the silver will turn black. Do not allow dry dishwasher detergent to come into contact with silver items as black spots will appear. Remove and, if necessary, dry silver cutlery immediately the dishwasher cycle has ended, to avoid staining and pitting from salt residue.

SEE ALSO

Cutlery, p.140

SILVER PLATE

Treat as for silver, but polish with less vigour as the plating is softer. Do not use dip solutions to clean silver plate that is wearing in patches as they can attack the base metal, and never leave silver-plated items in dip for more than 10 seconds. Avoid using abrasive cleaners, such as wadding, too frequently on silverplate.

■ **Worn silver plate:** items can be re-silvered, but this can be expensive. For companies who offer a re-plating service, contact the British Cutlery and Silverware Association.

Mirrors

Use a proprietary window cleaner and buff up with a lint-free cloth or chamois leather. Alternatively, use a mixture of 7.5ml (½ tbsp) vinegar or methylated spirits and 1 litre (1¾ pints) water. Do not let any liquid run between glass and backing or under the frame as this could eventually cause spots on the silver surface behind the glass.

To reduce misting in bathrooms and kitchens wipe with neat washing-up liquid and rub vigorously with kitchen paper. Or use an anti-mist product, available from cycle and car accessory shops.

Pictures and paintings

Cleaning and restoration should always be carried out by a conservator. Contact the Institute of Paper Conservation.

Sinks

Many sink manufacturers sell their own cleaning products and will send you instructions for care of your sink.

To prevent a build-up of grease in sinks or waste pipes flush once a week with a soda solution (150g/5oz soda crystals to 500ml/18fl oz hot water) or use a proprietary sink cleaner.

▶

SEE ALSO

Sinks and taps,
pp.62–63

COLOURED

As stainless steel, below. Do not leave tea, coffee and fruit juice to dry as they will stain sink. Soak stubborn stains in a solution of biological washing powder or well-diluted household bleach.

COMPOSITES

Wipe down with a damp cloth and washing-up liquid. If limescale leaves marks, or the surface is stained with tea or coffee, treat with Bar Keepers Friend, or remove with a scouring pad.

ENAMEL

As stainless steel, below, but limescale removers are not recommended. To remove limescale try using a plastic scourer, neat washing-up liquid and plenty of elbow grease.

STAINLESS STEEL

Wipe with a damp cloth and washing-up liquid solution or an anti-bacterial spray cleaner. For thorough cleaning, use a neat multi-purpose liquid or cream cleaner, rinse and dry. If you live in a hard water area, use a limescale cleaner or proprietary stainless steel cleaner once a week. Avoid using a plastic washing-up bowl as this can trap grit underneath and cause scratching. Neat bleach down the plug-hole can cause staining, so only use it diluted.

SEE ALSO

Bathroom taps, p.113

TAPS (INCLUDING CHROME, PLASTIC, GOLD AND BRASS FINISHES)

Clean regularly with a solution of washing-up liquid, rinse and dry. Do not use an abrasive cleaner. To remove heavy limescale deposits, soak a cloth in a proprietary descaler and wrap around tap. Do not leave for longer than the recommended time. Rinse thoroughly and dry. To remove limescale from chrome taps, rub with half a lemon, then rinse with water and buff dry.

Walls

CERAMIC WALL TILES

Wipe with a damp cloth and solution of washing-up liquid.
Buff dry. Stains can be rubbed with neat washing-up liquid.
To clean yellowed grouting, brush dilute bleach over the area
or use a whitening pen such as International Grout Pen.

PAINTWORK

As for ceramic wall tiles. For heavy soiling, wash with a
solution of sugar soap and rinse with clean water.

WASHABLE/VINYL PAPER

Sponge over with a solution of washing-up liquid, taking care
not to over-wet the surface. Any grease marks should always
be removed immediately.

Windows

Take down net curtains and blinds to avoid damage. Remove
ornaments from window-sills. Avoid cleaning windows on a
sunny day as the heat will make the glass dry too quickly and
cause it to smear. Make sure window is dry before cleaning.

SEE ALSO

PVCu Doors, p.118

FRAMES

Clean off mildew with an old rag dipped in fungicide such as
Mystox, to prevent mould growing back. Alternatively, try a
solution of bleach.

SEE ALSO

Mirrors, p.131

GLASS

Use a proprietary window cleaner or mix your own. For
grimy exteriors of windows, use 30ml (2 tbsp) ammonia
(available from chemists or hardware stores) mixed with

▶

4 litres (7 pints) water. For interior windows, use a weak solution of vinegar. Always use a lint-free cloth, or chamois leather. For a really good shine, buff window dry with crumpled newspaper, or rub window with a dry chamois leather or soft cloth.

SEE ALSO

Repairing window
leaks, p.225

SILLS

Check window sills regularly for rot, and replace any crumbling putty around glass panes with the correct type for either timber or metal.

Work surfaces

CERAMIC TILES

Treat as laminates, below.

- **Grouting:** if grouting becomes dirty, clean with a solution of one part bleach to four parts water. Use an old toothbrush to get between tiles. Wipe over with a damp cloth and allow to dry. Do not use a grouting whitener on matt tiles. Chipped tiles on work surfaces must be replaced.
- **Stains:** use a slightly abrasive cream cleaner such as Cif or Astonish on work-surface tiles, which are matt finished and therefore less likely to show scratches than glazed tiles.

LAMINATES (EG FORMICA)

Wipe down with washing-up liquid solution, or use an all-purpose cleaner with an anti-bacterial agent. Do not rinse.

- **Stains:** remove stains with neat multi-surface liquid cleaner, or cream cleaner, using a damp cloth. Rinse with clean water and allow to dry. For stubborn stains, use a slightly abrasive cream cleaner such as Cif or Astonish, or diluted bleach. On textured surfaces use a nylon bristle brush to get into the grain. Solvents will not damage laminates so stains such as felt-tip pen can be treated with methylated spirits, white spirit or nail polish remover.

■ **Chips and scratches:** these can be repaired with a laminate repairer and sealer such as ColorFill.

MAN-MADE SOLID SURFACES

Treat as laminates, above.

■ **Stains:** solvents can damage the surface after prolonged contact but can be used on stains if thoroughly rinsed afterwards. Stubborn stains can be rubbed gently with a mild abrasive cream cleaner such as Cif or Astonish, or bleach.

■ **Cuts and scratches:** these can be sanded away using medium-grade sandpaper, followed by fine-grade. Buff well afterwards to restore shine. In cases of severe damage, contact the manufacturer.

With light colours, you need to mop up any spills immediately so as to avoid staining.

NATURAL, SOLID SURFACES (INCLUDING GRANITE)

Treat as laminates, above. Pay particular attention to any joins in the surface. Wipe thoroughly with a soft, dry cloth. This sort of surface is difficult to stain and neat washing-up liquid should be sufficient to remove marks.

Damage contact the Stone Federation for specialist help.

STAINLESS STEEL

To remove finger marks, put a dab of cooking or baby oil on a clean cloth and rub whole surface, concentrating on marked areas. For thorough cleaning, wash stainless steel with a solution of washing-up liquid and buff dry with a soft cloth.

Household items

IN THIS CHAPTER YOU WILL FIND

This chapter contains advice on cleaning and maintaining household items and removing smells, and recommends the best cleaning products.

Barbecues

CASING
Wipe clean with washing-up liquid to remove grease marks. Do not use abrasive cleaners. If paintwork looks shabby, touch up aluminium or enamel with heat-resistant metal spray paint such as Plasti-Kote BBQ Spray Paint.

GRILLS
There are two main types: chrome-plated or porcelain-coated (which look black). Before using, wipe grills with cooking oil to prevent food sticking. Both types are easier to clean while still warm. To clean, use a solution of washing-up liquid in warm water. Avoid using abrasive cleaners or oven cleaners as they will damage the coating.

A brass-bristled brush will help remove food, but first rub food remains with crumpled aluminium foil, to avoid bristles clogging with grease. Some grills can be put in the dishwasher.

Basketware

If stains cannot be removed with normal washing, try gentle bleaching, then re-varnish if necessary. If a stain does not respond to bleaching, use a coloured polyurethane wood varnish to cover the stain.

▶

BAMBOO

A hollow cane, often split for weaving. Wipe clean with a solution of washing-up liquid, then dry with a cloth.

CANE

Imported baskets are usually made with split cane, and may have a light seal or varnish. Wipe down with water. For heavier dirt you may need to use a solution of washing-up liquid. Avoid using anything harsher, which may break through the seal and damage the cane underneath.

WILLOW

Mainly used for hampers and similar baskets. Usually unsealed. Clean as above. Do not over-wet or leave to soak.

Coffee makers

CAFETIÈRES

Remove plunger and unscrew rod from the filter assembly. Wash filter and glass beaker in hot, soapy water, or the dishwasher if appropriate. Stains on a bone china beaker can be removed with bicarbonate of soda. Buff brass or chrome frames with a soft cloth.

ELECTRIC FILTERS

Unplug and allow machine to cool down before cleaning. Wash filter holder and nylon filters by hand in warm, soapy water. Glass jugs can be washed in the dishwasher. Wipe body of machine with a damp cloth.

- **Descaling:** descale every 8-10 weeks in a hard-water area, or every six months in areas of moderately hard water. Only use proprietary descalers that state they are suitable for plastic kettles and/or coffee makers.

ESPRESSO/CAPPUCCINO MACHINES

Descale as for filter machines, above, but never try to force open the lid of the water tank. Immediately after use, wait until pressure has subsided and the lid comes off easily. Wash filter very carefully as espresso grains are extremely fine. Wash the steam/cappuccino nozzle thoroughly – most are removable and should be washed by hand.

TIP

If you have not used your cappuccino machine for a while, check the nozzle before you switch it on and, if necessary, unblock with a pin.

Computer equipment

KEYBOARDS

Unplug the computer from mains before cleaning. Turn upside down and shake to remove crumbs. Gently work over the keyboard with the brush attachment of your vacuum cleaner, using a low-suction setting if possible. If necessary, wet a cloth in a mild washing-up solution, wring it out well and wipe off any remaining dirt.

MONITORS

Use screen wipes and washes from computer and office supply shops including PC World, Staples and Office World.

Crockery

SEE ALSO

Dishwashers, pp.43–44

CHINA

Most china can be put in the dishwasher, with the exception of hand-painted and antique pieces and those with metallic trim. If china is labelled 'dishwasher-safe', use a detergent recommended by the china manufacturer. Load dishwasher so pieces do not touch one another, to avoid risk of chipping.

▶

- **Hand-washing:** use a hot solution of washing-up liquid – ideally in a plastic washing-up bowl – and a soft brush, cloth or mop. Avoid scouring pads, harsh abrasives, bleach or soda, which can damage the surface or dull patterns, especially gold and silver decoration. Rinse in warm water, drain, then dry and polish with a soft tea-towel. Do not stack wet pieces on top of one another as the footing is often unglazed and may scratch the piece underneath.
- **Stains:** if cups are stained, use a proprietary stain remover such as Oust Crockery & Cutlery Cleaner. Alternatively, try soaking in a solution of biological washing powder or bleach, rinsing thoroughly before use.

Cutlery

SEE ALSO

Silver/silver plate, Metals, pp.129–131

STAINLESS STEEL

Most stainless steel (except items with wooden and plastic handles) can be washed in the dishwasher, but rinse off food deposits first by hand, and remove immediately dishwasher cycle has ended. Never use rinse and hold cycle as humid atmosphere may cause 'rust' marks. Polish occasionally with a proprietary stainless-steel cleaner to maintain mirror finish. Wash thoroughly after polishing.

- **Stains:** hot grease may leave a stubborn rainbow-coloured mark, and mineral salts in tap water can cause a white film if not dried thoroughly. Acidic foods such as vinegar may also cause staining, while the humid atmosphere inside a dishwasher may pit the surface of the stainless steel. A proprietary stainless-steel cleaner will remove most marks. Wash items thoroughly after using a cleaning product.

 To remove tea stains from teaspoons soak overnight in a

proprietary stain cleaner such as Bar Keepers Friend or Jonelle Stainless Steel Cleaner, or add a teaspoon of biological washing powder to a mug of hot water. Rinse and wash thoroughly after soaking.

Decanters and carafes

To remove stains in the base fill with a warm solution of biological washing powder and leave to soak. If a stain is stubborn, try adding two tablespoons of rice to the liquid and gently swirl it round, to help loosen dirt. After cleaning, rinse decanter thoroughly in warm water. Stand it upside down in a wide-necked jug to drain and become thoroughly dry before storing.

 If a stopper is stuck, put on rubber gloves to protect your hands and help with grip. Wrap a very hot, damp cloth around the neck of the decanter to expand the glass, then slowly dribble some vegetable oil around the stopper. Wiggle and twist the stopper gently and it should come free.

Deep-fat fryers

Lids of most fryers are detachable, and some can be cleaned in the dishwasher. Clean the inside of the fryer every time the oil is changed (every six uses). Once the oil has been emptied, clean tank with a plastic scouring pad and washing-up liquid, taking care not to damage any non-stick coating. Wipe over outside of fryer with a damp cloth and non-abrasive cleaner.

 Always store fryer with lid slightly ajar to allow air to circulate, and wipe out before use.

Dishwashers

Switch off electricity supply before cleaning. Clean filters after each use. Spray arms should be cleaned in a solution of washing-up liquid – run water through the inlet of each spray arm to check holes are not blocked by food debris. Wipe exterior of machine with a damp cloth and solution of washing-up liquid. If machine will not be used for some time, leave door ajar to allow air to circulate. Occasionally use specialist products designed to de-scale and freshen machine, available from supermarkets.

Electric fires

FAN HEATERS

Keep grille clean and dust-free. If a heater stops working, turn it off and unplug it, then unscrew the grille and clean inside very gently with a soft brush.

RADIANT FIRES

These need to be kept sparkling clean so they reflect the maximum amount of heat, but take care not to knock the bars or the ceramic mounts when wiping the fireback.

Extractor fans

Unplug at the mains. Remove outer cover and wash in a warm solution of washing-up liquid. Rinse and dry. Wipe fan blades with a damp cloth wrung out in a solution of washing-up liquid – avoid getting them wet and ensure they are dry before replacing the fan cover.

Food mixers and processors

Disconnect from electrical supply before cleaning.

- **Pushers, lids and bowls:** these are usually dishwasher-safe.
- **Blades:** clean in a hot solution of washing-up liquid, using a kitchen brush. Wipe away food stains with a damp cloth and a very mild solution of bleach.

TIP

If stains from carrots or curry paste do not come off with normal washing try wiping bowl with kitchen paper moistened with vegetable oil. Repeat if necessary, then wash in hot soapy water to remove any greasy residue.

Freezers

Unplug freezer before cleaning and freshening the inside with a solution of warm water and bicarbonate of soda (1tbsp/15ml to 1¾ pints/1 litre). Remove stains using neat bicarbonate of soda on a damp cloth. Clean outside with a solution of washing-up liquid, rinse and wipe dry.

- **Defrosting:** some modern freezers are frost-free (though still need wiping out to freshen), but older freezers need defrosting when frost is about 3-4cm (1¼-1½in) thick. Remove food and store in a cold place, wrapped in newspaper and covered with an old blanket or duvet. Speed up defrosting by placing containers of hot, but not boiling, water in the cabinet. Scrape off ice with a wooden spoon or plastic scraper. When ice has melted, wipe freezer dry, replace food and switch on again.
- **To remove smells:** wash out, then wipe interior with a sterilising fluid or branded fridge-freezer cleaner such as Mr Muscle. Dry with a soft cloth and leave door open for as long as possible to allow air to circulate.

Fridges

Modern fridges have automatic defrost, but should be cleaned occasionally. Wipe all inside surfaces with a damp cloth, and dry well with a soft cloth. Alternatively, use a branded fridge cleaner. Clean outside with a solution of washing-up liquid, wiping metal parts with a damp cloth.

■ **To remove smells**: wipe down walls, shelves and door seal with a solution of 15ml (1tbsp) bicarbonate of soda to 1 litre (1¾ pints) warm water, or a disinfectant solution such as Milton.

TIP Help prevent smells returning by using a fridge deodoriser or leave bicarbonate of soda in an open container inside fridge.

Glassware

Glass engraving
Mappin and Webb,
and Thomas Goode &
Co Ltd, Directory
pp.271 and 272
Glass restoration
Facets, Redhouse
Glass Crafts, and
Wilkinson, Directory
pp.271 and 272
Decanters and
carafes, p.141

Glassware can become cloudy when washed in a dishwasher. Check rinse aid, salt and detergent levels are topped up then try washing glasses in the dishwasher using citric acid crystals, available from hardware stores and chemists. Fill the detergent dispenser with the citric acid and run the glass through a normal wash, without any detergent – the citric acid acts as a limescale remover, and will descale the dishwasher at the same time. Alternatively, try soaking glasses in a limescale remover solution (use a limescale remover suitable for plastic kettles).

Lead crystal Should always be washed by hand in warm water and washing-up liquid. Rinse in water of the same temperature, drain and dry with a soft cloth, preferably linen.

Griddle pans

If using a cast-iron pan for the first time, wash it in soapy water beforehand, rinse and dry thoroughly. Brush pan with cooking oil, then heat slowly until the pan is very hot but not smoking. Allow to cool and wipe out before use. After use, cool pan completely before washing or soaking, making sure you remove any bits of cooked food. It is especially important to keep cast-iron griddle pans clean – if debris is left to build up, the pan will start to smoke, and so will the food.

Ice cream makers

Many recipes use raw eggs, so good hygiene is essential. Wash bowls with a hot solution of washing-up liquid and always dry thoroughly before use.

Irons

Remove burnt-on or sticky deposits on the soleplate using a proprietary soleplate cleaner such as Vilene Iron Cleaner or Wenko Iron Cleaning Stick, or impregnated cloth from Minky, making sure you work in a well-ventilated room as cleaners can give off fumes. Alternatively, heat iron on a warm setting and rub across a damp, loosely-woven cloth or coarse towel held taut over the edge of the board. Gentle use of a moistened plastic scouring pad will remove dirt.

■ **Descaling:** use a proprietary scale remover, but check first with manufacturer's instructions – not all recommend this. Built-in anti-scale devices need replacing regularly.

Jewellery

SEE ALSO

Metals, p.128

Always wash jewellery in a plastic bowl with a cloth in the base. This will prevent pieces getting damaged, or falling down the plug-hole. Put the plug in as a precaution.

AMETHYSTS, DIAMONDS, RUBIES AND SAPPHIRES

Clean in a solution of washing-up liquid, scrubbing gently with a soft toothbrush or an eyebrow brush. Rinse in lukewarm water, then dip quickly into surgical spirit to remove any remaining detergent film before draining on absorbent paper and buffing with a chamois leather. These stones can also be cleaned by immersing in a proprietary jewellery care kit such as Town Talk Polish Gold and Jewellery Care Kit.

IMPORTANT

Do not store diamonds close together – although they are extremely hard they could still scratch one another.

EMERALDS

These are softer than other precious stones and can chip easily. Clean emeralds carefully in a warm solution of washing-up liquid.

MARCASITE

Never wash marcasite; instead, polish with a soft brush, then rub with a chamois leather.

PEARLS

Never wash in water. Oils from the skin help to maintain their gleam, so wear pearls as much as possible – but not while applying make-up, perfume or hairspray. Rub with a chamois leather from time to time.

TURQUOISE AND OPALS

These stones are porous, so never immerse in water. Polish with a soft, dry chamois leather and use a soft bristle brush to clean claws.

Jug blenders

Half-fill goblet with warm water and blend for 30 seconds.

Juicers

Clean immediately after use to avoid fruit and vegetable pulp sticking and staining. Using a kitchen brush or the brush provided, clean all parts with hot, soapy water, taking care when handling the grating sieve, which has sharp edges. Wipe the motor housing with a damp cloth and solution of washing-up liquid.

 If plastic has stained, use a damp cloth and mild solution of bleach or rub with vegetable oil. Rinse well.

Kettles

Descale regularly using a chemical descaler suitable for your kettle. Rinse kettle thoroughly and boil up several times with fresh water after treatment. Alternatively, cover the element with a solution of half distilled vinegar and half cold water and leave for a couple of hours.

Microwaves and combination ovens

Always disconnect before cleaning.

- **Interior:** models with an acrylic interior should be wiped out with a cloth and a hot solution of washing-up liquid. Alternatively, use a branded microwave cleaner. Never use anything abrasive. Some ovens with a stainless-steel interior can be cleaned with a normal oven spray-cleaner, but spray on to a cloth first to avoid spraying into vents.
- **Spillages:** these cook on to the glass plate, so wipe plate after use and clean occasionally in a hot solution of washing-up liquid, or in the dishwasher.
- **To remove smells:** open door when not in use, to circulate air. Place lemon slices in a basin of cold water and heat, uncovered, on high to boiling point, then for 20 minutes on medium so steam passes through the vents. Wipe dry.

Pans

ALUMINIUM

- **Uncoated, plain:** wash by hand, never in a dishwasher. If aluminium develops a black tarnish, remove by boiling up acidic foods such as rhubarb or a cut lemon in water. Wash pan thoroughly afterwards.
- **Hard-anodised:** clean in a hot solution of washing-up liquid. Never put in a dishwasher. If a brownish film develops on surface, remove with a mild abrasive cleaner.

CAST IRON

Wash uncoated cast iron saucepans by hand, never in a dishwasher. Dry thoroughly. Brush with a thin layer of vegetable oil to prevent rusting.

SEE ALSO

Griddle pans, p.145

SEE ALSO

Metals, copper and
Brass, p.128

COPPER

Wash in a hot solution of washing-up liquid. Clean as brass, washing the pan thoroughly afterwards.

ENAMELLED

Wash in a hot solution of washing-up liquid and dry immediately to prevent whitish film developing on surface. If enamel coating is thin, food may stick and burn – if so, soak pan and use a nylon scourer to remove deposit. Worn enamel may stain. Marks can be removed by boiling up a solution of biological washing powder in the pan.

GLASS-CERAMIC

Remove burnt-on food by soaking pan in a warm solution of washing-up liquid, then use a nylon scourer.

NON-STICK COATINGS

Wash, rinse and dry new pans before use. The non-stick coating may need to be lightly 'seasoned' by brushing interior with a thin layer of vegetable oil. Re-season after dishwashing. Remove burnt-on food deposits with a scourer specifically for non-stick surfaces.

IMPORTANT

Never use metal utensils or abrasive scourers on non-stick pans.

STAINLESS STEEL

Wash by hand or in dishwasher. Rainbow markings may develop over time – simply remove with a proprietary stainless steel cleaner. Pans subjected to too high a heat may develop brown marks on the exterior – these may come off with a proprietary cleaner such as Bar Keepers Friend or Jonelle Stainless Steel Cleaner.

■ **For severe burnt-on deposits:** in the saucepan bring to the ▶

boil a solution of biological washing powder (15ml/1 tbsp powder to 1.1 litres/2 pints water). Boil for 10 minutes, repeat if necessary, then wash thoroughly.

Pasta machines

Do not immerse in water as machine will rust. Use a dry pastry brush to remove any old pasta dough and wipe the machine with oil or a slightly damp cloth.

Tumble dryers

Clean filter after every use. Wipe exterior with a solution of washing-up liquid. Empty water container of condenser dryer after every use.

Vacuum cleaners

Use anti-static polish on plastic casing to avoid attracting dust. Follow manufacturer's instructions to clear blockages.

Vacuum flasks

To stop smells building up, store with the lid off, so air can circulate. If washing with washing-up liquid does not remove the smell of the last drink in the flask, fill with warm water and pop in a couple of denture-cleaning tablets or a few teaspoons of bicarbonate of soda. Leave to stand overnight, then wash with warm, soapy water and rinse thoroughly.

Vases

SEE ALSO

Glassware, p.144

Remove white deposits on the inside of cut-glass vases by filling vase with malt vinegar and a handful of dry rice. Swill it around and leave overnight. Rinse with hot, soapy water. If this doesn't work, you could try a limescale remover designed to descale plastic kettles – wear rubber gloves and apply neat, rubbing gently. Rinse immediately. Alternatively, try Magic Balls from Lakeland Ltd.

Washing machines

Clean clogged-up detergent drawers by removing and rinsing in a bowl of warm water. Wipe out drawer recess with a damp cloth. Check drain filter regularly if applicable. Clean outside of machine with a warm solution of washing-up liquid. Wipe with clean water and dry.

Waste bins

Use a disinfectant spray or solution of mild disinfectant and a damp cloth for regular cleaning. If the bin is soiled and stained, soak in a mild solution of bleach, then wash out and rinse with clean water.

■ **Wheelie bins:** wipe with solution of disinfectant. If necessary, use a proprietary bin freshener such as Bin Fresh.

Waste disposal units

A slice of lemon in the unit will reduce smells. Avoid using any drain-cleaning chemicals as they may damage unit.

Fabrics

IN THIS CHAPTER YOU WILL FIND

Here's how to clean, maintain and store all fabrics, with a guide to washing symbols and solutions to all your washday problems.

SEE ALSO

Directory, p.273, p.274 and p.272

For difficult stains on expensive garments, contact the Dry Cleaning Information Bureau or Leather Master (also for upholstery); for carpets and upholstery, contact Scotchcare Services or ServiceMaster.

BLEACHING, IRONING, DRY-CLEANING AND DRYING

⚠ cl	May be chlorine-bleached	◻	May be tumble dried
✕	Do not chlorine-bleach	⊙	May be tumble-dried using high heat setting
⌐	Hot iron – cotton, linen, viscose	⊙	May be tumble-dried using low heat setting
⌐	Warm iron – polyester mixtures, wool	⊠	Do not tumble-dry
⌐	Cool iron – acrylic, nylon, polyester	▯	Drip-dry recommended
Ⓟ	May be dry-cleaned (letters and/or bar underneath instruct dry-cleaner)	▥	Hang to dry
⊠	Do not dry-clean	⊟	Dry flat

Acetate

Man-made fibre often made into silk-like fabrics such as satin, taffeta and brocades and used for linings. Wash in warm water on delicates programme. Do not spin. Iron using cool setting. Avoid using acetone or vinegar to remove stains.

Acrylic

Often used for knitwear, as an alternative to wool. Wash in warm water using a synthetics programme with a short spin. Use fabric conditioner in last rinse to reduce static. Do not wring, and use a cool iron – not the steam setting. Pull back into shape when wet, and dry flat.

- **Curtains and soft furnishings:** dry-clean only.
- **Pile fabrics:** iron on wrong side. Brush pile with soft brush.

Angora

Soft rabbit wool used for jumpers, mohair fabrics and knitting yarns. Sometimes mixed with nylon. Always hand-wash, and treat as for wool.

- **Storage:** to prevent moulting, store in fridge.

Brocade

Heavy, stiff fabric with a raised pattern, often used for soft furnishings and upholstery. Can be made from cotton, silk, viscose or acetate. Dry-clean only. Use cool iron on reverse.

Broderie Anglaise

Traditional open-work embroidered fabric or lace, available in cotton or polyester. Wash according to fabric type. Wash delicate pieces by hand or in a muslin bag in the machine.

Calico

Plain, closely woven cotton, generally unbleached and coarse. Wash as for cotton. To whiten unbleached calico, add bleach to the first wash. Rinse thoroughly to remove smell.

Cambric

Traditionally a fine linen from France, but now generally cotton. Often used for table linen and handkerchiefs. Wash as for cotton. Iron when damp, using steam setting.

Canvas

Stiff, coarse cotton used for strengthening tailored garments, and making tents, handbags and shoes. Sponge or scrub soiled areas with a stain-removal bar or household block soap. Rinse with cool water.

- **Seating:** scrub heavy canvas with a nailbrush and household soap. Rinse by pouring water through the fabric. Dry naturally, supporting if necessary with a couple of chairs underneath. Specialist canvas cleaners are available from outdoor pursuits shops.
- **Shoes:** allow mud to dry before brushing off. Some canvas shoes can be machine-washed. Use a low-temperature synthetics programme. Alternatively, use an upholstery shampoo or proprietary cleaner for fabric shoes.

Cashmere

Light, soft and warm wool made from the hair of the Kash-mir goat. Hand-wash or dry-clean. Treat as for wool.

Chenille

Heavy fabric of cotton, viscose, wool or silk, with soft velvety pile. Wash according to fabric type, or dry-clean.

Chiffon

Finely woven sheer fabric made from cotton, silk or man-made fibres. Wash according to fibre type, or dry-clean. Do not wring or spin. Iron gently while damp using a cool iron.

Chintz

Tightly woven cotton, generally with a flowery design, used for furnishing fabrics. Some have a chemical glazed finish. Dry-clean only. Continual cleaning will remove the glaze.

Corduroy

Cotton or synthetic-mix woven ribbed fabric used for clothes and upholstery. Use a synthetics programme with minimum spin. Wash garments such as trousers inside-out. Iron on reverse while damp, using steam setting. Brush up pile gently.

STATIC ELECTRICITY
If fabric is washable, try adding fabric conditioner to the final wash to reduce static in clothes, or use anti-static tumble-dryer sheets. Avoid wearing tights under silk or synthetic trousers; moisturising your legs will also help. Wear a natural fibre garment between two synthetic ones, eg a cotton slip between a polyester skirt and polyamide tights. Anti-static sprays such as Go Stat, which are also suitable for use on carpets and curtains, are available from haberdashery sections of department stores such as John Lewis. If you regularly get 'shocks' when you touch things or people: keep your home humid by placing bowls of water near radiators as static is worse in a very dry atmosphere. Hand cream can also help reduce the feeling of shock.

Cotton

Available in different weights and qualities. Machine washable but may shrink or fade if washed at temperatures over 40°C. Iron while damp, using steam setting.

Crêpe de chine

Lightweight, slippery fabric traditionally made from silk but now mostly synthetic. Hand-wash according to fibre type. Cold rinse, roll in a towel to remove moisture. Iron on cool.

Damask

Heavy woven fabric with shiny thread. Made of silk, cotton, viscose or a combination. Often used for table linen. Wash according to fibre type. Dry-clean heavier items.

Denim

Hard-wearing twilled cotton. If not pre-shrunk, use a cool wash. Turn inside-out and wash separately as colour can run. Iron while still damp, using the maximum or steam setting.

Dralon

Trade name for an acrylic-fibre, velvet-type furnishing fabric.
- **Upholstery:** brush or vacuum regularly. Clean using a dry-foam upholstery shampoo.
- **Curtains:** dry-clean. Do not iron, but hang them immediately to avoid creasing.
- **Stains:** remove water-based stains immediately by blotting, then sponge with a weak solution of biological detergent. Rinse and blot dry. For other stains, try acetone applied with cotton wool. If in doubt, have it cleaned professionally.

Elastanes
and Lycra A synthetic alternative to rubber, these keep their elasticity
well. Machine-wash at low temperatures using a delicates
programme, or hand-wash in warm water, rinse, and use a
short spin or roll in a towel. Do not tumble-dry.

Felt
Thick, non-woven material made from matted wool fibres.
Should always be dry-cleaned.

Flannel
Woven wool or wool and cotton blend, mainly used for suits.
Dry-clean suits and expensive items, otherwise treat as wool.

Fur fabric
Made from polyamide, viscose, cotton, acrylic or polyester.
Dry-clean cotton and viscose; wash others as nylon/
polyamide, shaking well before allowing to dry naturally. For
light soiling, sponge area with a warm solution of non-
biological washing powder, rinse and towel dry. Brush
straight-pile fabric while still damp. Between washings, brush
pile with a medium to hard brush.

Gaberdine
Made from wool, cotton or either blended with man-made
fibres. Often used for coats and suits. Dry-clean only.

Georgette

Fine, sheer fabric made from cotton, silk, wool or man-made fibres. Dry-clean natural fabrics. Wash man-made fabrics according to fibre type.

Gingham

Checked or striped cotton or polyester-cotton fabric. Check for colourfastness, then wash according to fibre type. Steam-iron while damp.

Grosgrain

Fine, ribbed fabric of silk or man-made blends. Wash according to fibre type, or dry-clean.

Jersey

Stretchy knitted fabric of wool, silk, cotton or man-made fibres. Wash according to fibre type, or dry-clean. Short spin. Dry flat, pulling to shape while wet. Steam-iron on reverse.

Lace

Cotton, polyester, polyamide or a combination. Wash according to fibre type, using a gentle non-biological powder. If washing in a machine, place in a muslin bag or pillowcase. Iron while damp, on the wrong side, pulling to shape.

- **Antique lace:** Wash by hand with mild detergent, dry flat. Pin delicate pieces to a padded board covered with cotton and sponge with a mild detergent solution such as Woolite or Persil Silk and Wool. Rinse with cold water. Dry-clean precious items, or consult the Royal School of Needlework.

Leather

SEE ALSO

Luggage and bags,
p.181; Nubuck,
p.162;
Suede, p.165;
Sheepskin, p.164

Chamois Hand-wash in a warm soapflake solution, squeezing to release dirt. Rinse in a warm solution to which 5ml (1tsp) olive oil has been added, to retain soft texture. Squeeze out moisture and pull to shape. Hang to dry away from direct heat. Scrunch up leather during drying to maintain flexibility.
■ **Storage:** store damp in a polythene bag.

Clothing 'Washable' leather clothing should be sponged, never immersed in water. Treat new or newly cleaned clothes with waterproof spray. All clothing should be professionally cleaned every three to four years, re-tinted and re-oiled.
■ **Soiling:** remove surface soiling from washable leathers with a soapy sponge – use glycerine soap or soapflakes. Wipe with a clean damp cloth and hang to dry.
■ **Storage:** store on a padded hanger in a cotton cover.

Furniture Dust regularly and occasionally apply hide food, available from specialist outlets or department stores, to prevent leather from drying out and protect against stains. Remove all-over grime by wiping with a soft, damp cloth. Professionally clean obvious stains. Site leather furniture away from radiators or other direct heat; it can encourage cracking.

Gloves Wearing the gloves, wash in a warm soapflake solution. Rub hands together gently. Remove and allow to dry. When nearly dry, put on to restore shape. Do not rinse doeskin gloves as the soap keeps them supple – after washing, press between two towels to remove moisture, dry naturally.

Patent If it becomes very cold it will crack. Dust with a soft cloth and apply patent-leather dressing when dull.

■ **Storage:** apply thin layer of petroleum jelly (Vaseline) all over, and wipe off before use. Use shoe trees or stuff with paper.

SEE ALSO

Companies that dye shoes
Georgina's Shoes, and Ivory, Directory p.271

Shoes and handbags When new, apply a waterproof protector.

■ **Shoes:** clean regularly with recommended shoe polish to clean and maintain dye colour, and cover scuff marks. If shoes get really wet, dry out at room temperature in a well-ventilated spot. Stuff with paper to help retain shape, or use a shoe tree. Never dry leather shoes in front of a radiator.

■ **Handbags:** these need similar care. Do not use pigmented polishes, which will rub off on to clothing.

■ **To remove grease and oils:** coat stain with thin layer of rubber adhesive, leave on for 24 hours, then roll off adhesive. Treat with hide food. Alternatively, use a proprietary cleaner such as Lord Sheraton Leather Shine (available from Safeway, Allders and CWS), testing first for colourfastness.

Linen

Woven fabric from flax fibres. Hot wash and spin-dry. Hang to dry. Garments with special anti-crease finishes should be dry-cleaned. Iron on the reverse while still damp, using a hot steam iron. Starch occasionally to give fabric a bit of body. Rub a stain-removal bar along dampened lines before washing.

■ **Storage:** stored linen can become soiled along the crease lines.

Metallic yarn

Includes lamé and woven brocade-type fabrics that contain metallic thread. Should always be dry-cleaned.

Microfibres

Fabrics made from ultra-fine polyester or polyamide yarns. Air pockets become trapped between the fibres making fabrics soft and light. Machine-wash using a 40°C wash programme. Minimum spin. Warm or steam iron.

Milium

Metallic-coated fabric used for its insulating properties, particularly in curtain linings and ironing boards. If making curtains, the metallic side should face inwards. Dry-clean.

Mohair

Light, woven fabric made from hair of the Angora goat, often mixed with other fibres. Hand-wash and treat as wool.

Moire

Traditionally made from silk, but now often from synthetics. Heavy weights are used for furnishings and lighter weights for ballgowns. Watermarked surface is easily damaged by water, so dry-clean only. Do not use a steam iron.

Muslin

This is an open-weave sheer cotton. Hand-wash carefully in warm water. Do not spin. Dry flat. Iron muslin while damp using a medium setting.

Nubuck

Made from cow leather, like suede, but is then buffed to a finer velvet pile. To clean use specialist nubuck and calf-leather cleaners, which require no brushing. Do not use suede shampoos or brushes as they will damage pile.

Percale

Finely woven cotton or polyester-cotton blend often used in bedding. Can also be glazed. Wash according to fibre type.

Polyamide and Nylon

Lightweight, non-absorbent man-made fibre that is elastic and strong even when it is wet. Flame resistant, but melts instead. Wash in hand-hot water, or on a 40°C delicates programme in the washing machine. Use fabric conditioner to reduce static. Cold rinse, short spin and drip-dry. Cool iron if necessary. Absorbs dye easily, so wash colours separately. Avoid bleach or direct heat or sunlight.

Polyester and Trevira

Synthetic fibre often combined with cotton. Wash using 40°C or 50°C synthetics programme with a short spin. Use fabric conditioner in final rinse. Can be tumble-dried. Treat grease stains immediately by soaking in a biological powder. Hand-wash pleated items and allow to drip dry, preferably outside on a clothes-line.

Poplin

Closely woven cotton, can be made from viscose, silk or wool. Wash or clean according to its fibre type.

PVC

SEE ALSO

Mildew, p.200

Strong plastic material or coating, used for upholstery, tablecloths, shower curtains etc. Sponge off dirty marks with warm water. Use a dilute solution of washing-up liquid for all-over soiling. Where applicable, hand-wash in warm water and drip dry, preferably outside on a clothes-line. Do not apply heat as it will melt. Do not dry-clean.

Satin

Smooth fabric with a short nap made from silk, cotton, polyester, polyamide or acetate. Used for dress fabrics, linings and lingerie. Wash according to fibre type. Iron on reverse side while still damp until dry. Dry-clean heavier items.

Shantung

Originally slubbed Chinese silk, now also made from acetate or polyamide. Wash according to fibre type.

Sheepskin

Coats When new, apply a protective spray to help prevent marking. Have professionally cleaned regularly. To clean small areas of skin, use a suede cleaner, but test first. Marks on the wool side can be freshened by using a dry shampoo for hair.

Rugs Wash at home using a solution of soap flakes if the wool pile is quite short. Or have it cleaned professionally.

Silk

Luxury fibre made from the cocoon of the silkworm. Wash using a mild liquid detergent designed for hand-washing, but never hand-wash items labelled dry-clean only. Avoid biological detergents, heat and washing soda, which can damage fibres. Do not rub or wring fabric. Use fabric conditioner in final rinse, then roll up in a clean dry towel and squeeze lightly to remove surplus water. Silk is not very colourfast so after the final rinse, try soaking in a solution of 10ml (2 tsp) vinegar to 3 litres (5¾ pints) water. Leave for 3 minutes, then dry. Iron while still damp with a warm iron.

- **Taffetas, brocades, printed silks:** dry-clean only.
- **Stains:** wash after each wear as perspiration stains may become impossible to remove. For fatty stains, try a detergent designed for coloureds. Have all other stains professionally removed.

Suede

Clothes Treat new or newly cleaned suede with a waterproof spray to prevent colour rubbing off, but test first. Wipe over dirty or rain-spotted suede with a clean damp cloth and allow to dry naturally. Brush frequently with a wire brush or suede block. For serious discoloration, it is best to have the item professionally cleaned.

Shoes Treat new shoes with protective suede spray. When necessary clean with a nailbrush and clean soapy water. Rinse and blot dry. If shoes get wet, allow to dry naturally, then use a suede brush to remove dust and raise pile.

Taffeta

Crisp, closely woven shiny material made from a variety of fibres including silk, acetate, viscose, polyester or polyamide. Dry-clean. Iron on reverse side.

Towelling

SEE ALSO

Washing problem solver (fabric harshess), p.170

Looped pile fabric usually made from cotton. Machine-wash on a cotton programme. Wash dark colours separately. Wash nappies on a hot wash, add fabric conditioner to final rinse. If towels go stiff, soak overnight in a solution of water softener then machine wash with maximum detergent. Tumble dry. Use fabric conditioner every third wash to keep soft.

Tulle

Fine, sheer net-like fabric of silk, cotton, viscose, polyamide or other fibres, used for evening and bridal wear. Dry-clean silk; hand-wash other fibres following instructions for fibre type. Starch cotton tulle if it becomes limp. Nylon and viscose tulle can be stiffened with a gum arabic solution, such as Harvest Gold, available from health food shops.

Tweed

Woven woollen fabric available in different weights. Imitations also made in polyester and acrylic. Dry-clean.

Velour

Pile fabric similar to velvet, usually made of acrylic but may be other man-made fibres, cotton or silk. Dry-clean or wash according to fibre type. Iron with a cool iron on reverse.

Velvet

Once a silk or cotton cut-pile fabric, but now also made from man-made fibres such as viscose, polyamide and polyester. Treat according to fibre, or dry-clean. Shake periodically while drying and smooth pile with a soft cloth or velvet brush to restore pile. Use steam to remove between-wear creases. Iron with pile face down on a soft cloth or towel.

Viscose (also called Rayon)

Fibre made from the pulp of eucalyptus and spruce wood, used on its own or in blends. Wash with care at low temperatures. To discourage creasing, use a short spin when washing and do not wring. Iron while damp on steam setting.

Viyella

Brand name for lightweight wool-and-cotton blend fabric. Hand-wash in hand-hot water. Do not spin. Remove water by squeezing gently or rolling in a towel. Warm iron while damp on reverse.

Wool

Hand-wash carefully in warm water, using a gentle detergent. Do not rub, wring or twist. Dry flat between two towels, pulling gently to correct shape while damp. Never tumble-dry. If label specifies it as machine-washable, use the woollens programme, which has reduced agitation and a very short spin.

- **Oiled wool:** Guernsey sweaters should be washed in warm water using well-dissolved soapflakes. Oiled wool sweaters can be re-oiled – check with manufacturer.

WASHING SYMBOLS

Symbol	Accompanying wording	Washing temperatures Machine	Hand	Examples
95	'Wash in cotton cycle/programme' or 'wash as cotton'	Very hot 95°C Normal action, rinse, spin	Hand-hot 50°C	White cotton and linen without special finishes
60	'Wash in cotton cycle/programme' or 'wash as cotton'	Hot 60°C Normal action, rinse, spin	Hand-hot 50°C	Cotton, linen or viscose without special finishes where colours are fast at 60°C
50	'Wash in synthetics cycle/programme' or 'wash as synthetics'	Hot 50°C Reduced action, cold rinse, reduced spin or drip dry	Hand-hot 50°C	Nylon, polyester/cotton mixtures; polyester, cotton and viscose with special finishes; cotton/acrylic mixtures
40	'Wash in cotton cycle/programme' or 'wash as cotton'	Warm 40°C Normal action, rinse, spin	Warm 40°C	Cotton, linen or viscose where colours are fast at 40°C but not at 60°C
40	'Wash in synthetics cycle/programme' or 'wash as synthetics'	Warm 40°C Reduced action, cold rinse, reduced spin	Warm 40°C	Acrylics, acetates and triacetate including mixtures with wool; polyester/wool blends
40	'Wash in wool cycle/programme' or 'wash as wool'	Warm 40°C Much-reduced action, normal rinse, spin	Warm 40°C	Wool, wool mixed with other fibres; silk and delicate fabrics
(hand)	'Hand-wash (do not machine-wash)'	See garment label		

Check care labels on clothes and household linen and use appropriate settings. With a mixed load of fibres, use the lowest recommended temperature. Two sets of symbols are shown as old ones can still be found on some items. For advice on fabric care, contact the Home Laundering Consultative Council (HLCC).

WASHDAY PROBLEM SOLVER

PROBLEM	CAUSE	CURE	PREVENTION
Bobbling on cotton and synthetic blends	Abrasion of the fibres from normal wear	Pick off bobbles by hand or with sticky tape. Alternatively, use a safety razor or specific de-fuzzing gadget	Difficult to prevent, but try washing garments inside out and use a fabric conditioner
Dye transfer from other garments (colour runs)	Non-colourfast items have been washed with paler items at too high a temperature. Excess dye from dark-coloured items has leached to other items in the washload	**White wash:** check item is not nylon and does not have a 'do not bleach' symbol (see p.153). If not, soak in a weak solution of household bleach (20ml/¾fl oz bleach per 5 litres/9 pints water) for 15 minutes. Rinse thoroughly by hand or use a rinse programme on washing machine. Repeat as necessary. **Coloureds:** try a proprietary colour run remover, but test on a hidden area first as it may affect colour	Sort your load carefully and test for colour fastness (see The 10 Golden Rules of Stain Removal, p.187). Always wash dark colours separately at first, and do not use too high a temperature for non-colourfast items. Do not mix whites and coloured items
Excessive creasing	Incorrect wash programme, over-drying or overloading machine	Reduce temperature, or wash with smaller loads. Use the specific synthetics programmes which have reduced drum agitation and shorter spin cycles at lower speeds	Follow care labelling. Creasing of synthetics occurs if too high washing and drying temperatures are used

►

WASHDAY PROBLEM SOLVER

PROBLEM	CAUSE	CURE	PREVENTION
Fabric harshness, particularly towels	Over-drying natural fibres; continual under-dosing with detergent, allowing mineral salts to build up; or inadequate rinsing of the washload	**Under-dosing:** soak in a solution of water softener (eg Calgon), using 30ml (2 tbsp) softener to 4 litres (7 pints) water. Also, run machine empty, using the hottest programme with the recommended dose of detergent containing a bleaching agent to remove any calcium build-up within the machine **Inadequate rinsing:** wash fabrics at as high a temperature as possible without any detergent. Add 1 cup/190ml white vinegar to the drawer dispenser of machine	Follow manufacturer's pack recommendation for dosage. Increase this if the items are heavily soiled. If drying natural fibre garments on a radiator or in a tumble dryer, remove them before fully dry to prevent removal of natural moisture within the fibres
Greying of white cottons	Dirt and soiling removed during washing have re-deposited on to clothes as a very thin uniform layer, making whites appear slightly grey and coloureds dull. This occurs if insufficient detergent is used	Re-wash using the maximum dose of detergent and wash temperature Soak in a bleach solution. Rinse thoroughly	Follow manufacturer's recommended dosing instructions and wash programme. Do not overload machine

WASHDAY PROBLEM SOLVER

PROBLEM	CAUSE	CURE	PREVENTION
Patchy colours or staining	Chemicals in the wash water. Light patches on bedding and nightwear can be caused by some skin creams, or neat, heavy-duty powders in direct contact with damp, non-colourfast fabric	Re-washing may remove some types of staining. If dyes have been affected, the problem is permanent Redye clothes. Companies that dye clothes: Giltbrook cleaners and Dyers and Harry Berger, Directory, p.271	Avoid fabrics touching offending chemicals or neat detergents
Rucking of collars and shirt-fronts	Collars and bands have facings with layers of different sorts of fabrics to stiffen them. These can shrink at different temperatures when washed, causing puckering of top fabric. Using cotton thread to sew synthetic fabrics can also cause puckering as cotton shrinks	May be irreversible. However, try steam-ironing garment while damp and carefully pulling offending layers into shape	Dry-clean items or wash in cool water to avoid shrinkage
Shrinking and felting of wool	Too-high wash temperatures, excessive agitation, tumble-drying or direct heat when drying	None. It is irreversible	Only machine-wash if label states it is machine-washable. If in doubt, hand-wash. Never tumble-dry wool
White/grey specks or streaks	Hard-water deposits that are present in the local water supply	Re-wash using maximum dosage of detergent. You may have to soak the load in a water softener	Increase dosage of detergent. In very hard-water areas, carry out an idle wash periodically with just detergent and no load, to help reduce scale build-up

Soft furnishings and fabric items

IN THIS CHAPTER YOU WILL FIND

Here we give cleaning and care advice for soft furnishings and fabric items, including the best storage methods and recommended fabric deodorisers.

Bedding

SEE ALSO

Blankets, p.176

BABIES' BEDDING

To help keep dustmites at bay, vacuum cot every few months. Most baby bedding can only be washed at 40°C which, according to Allergy UK, will not kill dustmites; however, they say that putting bedding or other warm-wash fabric in the freezer overnight before washing will do the trick. If it is not practical to freeze bedding before laundering, use Con-ex, a cold water wash additive that you add to your ordinary detergent to kill dustmites – it is suitable for washing any delicate fabric you cannot wash at 60°C.

DUVETS AND QUILTS

Never dry-clean feather duvets or quilts, or any heavily-wadded items. Wash in a large launderette machine, checking first that there are no holes or weak points in casing fabric – repair and patch first where necessary. Use one-third the usual amount of detergent. Shake out to stop it going lumpy, then dry thoroughly and leave to air for a day. You may be able to dry-clean thin polyester duvets but always check the manufacturer's instructions.

SEE ALSO

Removing stains and marks, p.186

■ **Spills and stains:** mop up spills immediately to avoid them soaking though the filling. If casing has become stained, ease the filling away from that area and tie it off with an elastic band or string. Sponge this area first with cold water, ▶

then with a mild detergent solution, taking care not to over-wet. For stubborn marks, soak in a biological detergent solution.

■ **Maintenance:** air frequently to keep filling fluffy and dry. Shake occasionally to re-distribute filling. Store duvets and quilts in a cool place – on a spare bed is ideal. Fold loosely to store in a cupboard.

ELECTRIC BLANKETS

Clean and service every three years – manufacturers carry out servicing, and may also offer cleaning services. Never have electric blankets dry-cleaned. Blankets that have detachable control panels are usually washable (check with manufacturer first) – if so, use a little washing-up liquid and water on a sponge, avoiding over-wetting. Dry naturally and make sure it is completely dry before use. To freshen up, use a little talcum powder, then brush away with a clothes brush. Some electric blankets, such as those made by Dreamland, are now machine-washable.

■ **Safety:** discard blanket if it becomes frayed, or if you detect scorch marks. Never use an electric blanket if it is damp. Regularly examine the wiring inside by holding blanket up to the light to make sure wires do not overlap, and check the flex and connections regularly. Make sure your electric blanket lies flat.

■ **Storage:** lay it flat under the mattress or on a spare bed, or roll (don't fold) if necessary.

FUTONS

Futons filled with cotton or wool/cotton fillings should not be washed or dry-cleaned – it is worth buying a futon with a removable cover that can be removed for washing or dry-cleaning. Only polyester-filled futons can be washed.

- **Spills:** treat immediately – isolate the area and spot-clean with water or very mild detergent solution.
- **Care:** air futon regularly, and turn weekly to prevent the filling from compacting.

MATTRESSES

- **Foam:** never turn foam mattresses with a layered construction. Single-layered mattresses should be turned regularly. Vacuum using crevice tool.
- **Spring interior:** to help filling settle, turn over or swing round to reverse head and foot frequently when new, then every three months, though some of the newest mattresses do not need turning (follow manufacturer's instructions). Occasionally brush mattress and base to remove fluff and dust. Vacuum the mattress if necessary using low suction and the appropriate nozzle.
- **Care:** consider buying separate mattress covers, which are removed for washing. (For information on keeping dustmites at bay, see Babies' bedding, p.173.)

PILLOWS

It is best to have pillows professionally cleaned as they may become lumpy and hard when washed. Never use a launderette dry-cleaning machine because chemical fumes are difficult to remove. If you want to try cleaning them yourself, here are some guidelines.

- **Foam:** sponge in warm, soapy water once a year. Rinse well, removing excess water with absorbent towel. Do not wring. Dry away from direct heat and sunlight.
- **Natural filling** air regularly outdoors in summer. Do not dry-clean. Wash in washing machine, checking first that machine can take weight. Hang outdoors to dry thoroughly, shaking occasionally – this may take several days. Air

▶

thoroughly before re-using.

- **Polyester/hollowfibre:** machine-wash using wool programme and a third of the normal quantity of detergent. Spin, then tumble-dry.
- **Care:** plump up pillows frequently to avoid filling compacting. Keep laundering to a minimum as it can reduce the life of pillow.

Blankets

SEE ALSO

Electric blankets,
p.174

Usually made from wool, but cotton and synthetics also available. Most wool blankets should be dry-cleaned. Synthetic and cotton blankets are usually machine-washable, but check label first and make sure dry blanket will fit in your machine. Blankets can be hand-washed in the bath. Dry naturally away from direct heat.

- **Care:** rest blankets occasionally to help prolong their life. When not in use, wash, clean, air and store sealed in a polythene bag in a cool cupboard.

Blinds (fabric)

AUSTRIAN/FESTOON

Vacuum on a low-suction setting using the upholstery tool. Blinds may need the occasional wash or dry-clean.

SEE ALSO

Blinds, wood and
metal, p.114

ROLLER

Vacuum using the upholstery tool, or use a soft brush. If blind is waterproof, remove deeper dirt by taking it down and sponging the fabric, using an upholstery shampoo or a proprietary roller-blind cleaner, such as Copes Blind Cleaner, from department stores or specialist curtain shops. Avoid over-wetting, and rehang while still damp.

TIP

To check blind is waterproof, sprinkle a little water on the surface – if it sinks in, the fabric is not waterproof.

- **If blind does not wind properly:** re-tension by pulling the blind halfway down, then remove from the brackets and rewind by hand. Pull down and repeat if necessary.
- **If blind is badly spattered:** if drop is longer than the window requires, salvage the blind by detaching fabric and turning it round, provided it is plain or has a non-directional fabric. Take down the blind, unpin it from roller and remove batten at the base. Cut away damaged area and tack the new end to the roller. Make a new slot for the batten and re-hang blind.

Carpets

SEE ALSO

Upholstery, pet hairs, p.184; Vacuum cleaners, p.106; Static electricity, p.156; Carpets, p.45, Animal stains, p.189

Vacuum regularly to remove embedded dust and grit that could damage the fibres, and to keep the pile in good condition. For thorough cleaning you can use a 3-in-1 cleaner, such as a Vax, or hire one of the following:

- A manual or electric carpet shampooer that dispenses dry-foam shampoo which forms a powder when dry, absorbing dirt. This is then vacuumed away.
- A steam cleaner that sprays hot water and a cleansing agent under pressure into the carpet, then extracts it immediately together with any dirt.

- **Professional carpet cleaning:** for stubborn stains it's worth having a carpet professionally cleaned. Choose a member of the National Carpet Cleaners' Association, but do get several quotes and compare prices. If you have a problem with the cleaner, the NCCA has an arbitration scheme.
- **Care:** most carpets are supplied with care instructions. If not, contact the National Carpet Cleaners' Association for ▶

SEE ALSO

Removing stains and
marks, pp.186–213

advice on how to clean.

- **Stains and spills:** tackle immediately. Use the lather from a solution of dry-foam shampoo, or use a carpet-spotting kit available from hardware and department stores.
- **To raise pile of crushed carpet:** cover the area with a damp cloth and hold a hot iron over the cloth. Alternatively, rub with ice-cubes in a plastic bag. In both cases, brush up to lift pile when dry,
- **To help get rid of smells on carpets and soft furnishings:** try a proprietary deodoriser such as Neutradol or Febreze.

Christening gowns

See Wedding dresses, p.185.

Curtains

SEE ALSO

Static electricity,
p.156,
Fabrics, care and
cleaning, pp.152–167

Some fabrics can be washed, although weight and size of curtains may make this impossible. As a general rule, the following fabrics should be dry-cleaned only: velvets, velours, chenilles, tapestries and brocades; all fabrics containing wool or silk; and all interlined curtains. Whatever the fabric, curtains should be thoroughly cleaned every few years – dirty curtains will eventually rot and need to be replaced.

FABRIC

Brush down monthly, using the upholstery nozzle of your vacuum cleaner, on a low-suction setting. Alternatively, use a soft, long-handled brush.

Thorough cleaning (washable fabrics)

- Remove all hooks and curtain weights and loosen heading tape. Let down hem if the fabric is likely to shrink. Shake curtains to remove dust.
- Soak curtains in cold water first. Then wash carefully, according to the type of fabric. If hand-washing, make sure the detergent is thoroughly dissolved before immersing curtains. Do not rub or wring. Rinse thoroughly. Squeeze out as much water as possible, or use a short spin. If machine-washing, use a 'delicates' programme.
- Iron curtains while still damp. Work lengthways, on the wrong side, stretching fabric gently to avoid puckering of the seams. Hang the curtains while slightly damp so they drop to the right length.
- Clean curtain tracks, windows and sills before re-hanging.

NET

Wash frequently as net curtains tend to hold on to dirt once soiled. Wash separately in hot water, but do not exceed the recommended washing and drying temperatures as nets will become permanently creased. Rinse in cold water.

- **Whitening:** use a proprietary whitener, such as Dylon Net Curtain Whitener, available from supermarkets, department stores and hardware stores. Alternatively, try soaking nets in biological detergent.
- **Re-hanging:** re-hang while damp, running a thin rod through the hem until the net curtains are dry, to help them keep their shape.

Electric blankets

See Bedding, p.174.

Embroidery

Lampshade re-covering
Horrocks Shades, Directory p.271

Embroidery silks and wools are often not colourfast. Check by pressing a wad of white cotton fabric against the stitches in a hidden area, and ironing over it gently. Dry-clean if not colourfast, otherwise hand-wash and treat as wool. The Royal School of Needlework can restore valuable pieces.

Lampshades

FABRIC

Clean using a vacuum cleaner fitted with a dusting brush, reducing strength of suction if possible. Spots can be treated with a solution of washing-up liquid, but take great care –

FABRIC DEODORISERS	
ODOUR	RECOMMENDED PRODUCTS
Cooking smells and smoke	Deofab Febreze Extra Strength FreshenUp Refresh X=O
Doggy smells	None worked
Pet's urine	FreshenUp Sta-Kill X=O
Sweaty trainers	Deofab Febreze Extra Strength X=O

this could remove the surface finish, cause watermarks or dissolve glues holding the shade together.

■ **To remove fly specks:** try an aerosol stain remover such as K2r, available at John Lewis, Morrisons and some chemists. If that doesn't work, try biological washing powder in warm water (do not use on silk, and cover trimmings to prevent them getting wet).

 Use a soft toothbrush to work solution over the stains from both sides. Repeat with clean water. Blot and allow to dry naturally away from direct heat.

Luggage and bags

Because luggage materials differ, try a patch test before using any of these methods.

COTTON/COTTON TAPESTRY
Remove marks or grease by sponging a very weak solution of biological washing detergent on affected areas. Rinse by dabbing with clean water.

Leather, pp.160–161

LEATHER
■ **Handbags:** keep clean and supple with a leather shoe and bag polish.
■ **Suitcases:** after use, brush off loose dirt and wipe luggage with a damp cloth that has been rubbed over a tablet of glycerine soap; alternatively, use a very weak, warm soapflake solution but wring out cloth well before use. Finish with a cloth wrung out in clear water, then pat dry. Apply hide food occasionally. Do not over-wet.

▶

SYNTHETIC

- **Plastic/vinyl (soft) handbags:** if wet, allow to dry naturally and then brush with a stiff brush, then wipe with a very dilute solution of glass cleaner such as Sparkle. Remove stains with a solution of washing powder, or a Vanish soap, sponged on affected area. Once stain has gone, wipe with clean water and dry.
- **Plastic/vinyl (hard) handbags:** as soft bags, but it is best to avoid glass cleaner – it will lift the stain but you will have to treat the whole panel as it leaves a film on the surface.
- **Polypropylene suitcases:** clean with a weak, warm solution of washing-up liquid. Wipe dry.
- **Polyester sports/travel bags:** wipe with a cloth and a weak solution of washing-up liquid. Dry thoroughly.

Rainwear

Some items can be machine-washed. Bulky items and those with protective finishes should be dry-cleaned. Rubberised macs should be scrubbed with a soft brush and detergent solution. Wipe with a damp cloth and dry with a towel.

Soft toys

Hand-wash using a mild detergent solution. Rinse well. Wrap in a towel to soak up excess moisture, but avoid squeezing. Shake to distribute filling.

Straw hats

- **To remove dust:** use the upholstery tool on the vacuum cleaner, on a low suction. Protect trimmings with a cloth.
- **To rescue a squashed hat:** use a fairly hot iron either on steam

mode or with a damp cloth between the straw and the iron, making sure you don't let the iron lie on the straw. Rest the brim on the ironing board, underside up, and press, moving it round as you go. If the hat has a flat top, cut a piece of cardboard to that shape and place it inside, then pack with crumpled newspaper before pressing. If it has a round crown, a pudding basin will make a better base to press against. Once you have damp-pressed the whole hat, gently finish off with a dry iron, again taking care not to leave the hot iron in contact with the straw.

Sunshades

See Canvas, p.155.

Tapestry

Never get tapestry wet. To remove the dust that builds up on an unglazed tapestry, use the suction tool on your vacuum cleaner with a piece of fine muslin fastened over the end to avoid disturbing the fibres. If the fabric has become greasy, scatter a little bran over it, then gently vacuum it off. The bran should absorb the grease without leaving any floury deposit behind – it's also a good way of removing any general grubbiness from sections of bare canvas. If you prefer to have your tapestries professionally cleaned, contact the Royal School of Needlework.

Ties

Most are polyester, wool or silk. Spray new ties with a fabric protector. To check that it won't leave a mark, test it on the back first and leave to dry before doing front. To remove stains, try a dry-cleaning spray or have tie professionally cleaned. To iron, place tie wrong side up on ironing board and ensure interlining is flat. Slip a cardboard shape inside wide end so you press it without causing an imprint of the seam. Press over a damp cloth to avoid scorching.

Trainers

SEE ALSO

Leather, gloves, p.160

Made from a range of materials including plastic, leather, latex, canvas and other synthetic fabrics. Rinse off mud after use, using the back of an old knife in the tread. Pack with newspaper and let shoes dry naturally at room temperature. Clean by wiping over with a soft cloth soaked in a detergent solution. Only machine-wash if specifically recommended.
- **Care:** do not leave in bright sunlight, or keep damp shoes in a bag.

Upholstery

SEE ALSO

Leather, p.160;
Fabric deodorisers,
p.180, Animal
stains, p.189

Dust often using the brush attachment and crevice tool of the vacuum cleaner. Turn removable cushions weekly to ensure even wear. Wash or dry-clean loose covers according to fabric type. If washed, replace covers before completely dry to re-shape and prevent shrinkage. Iron in position, using a cool iron on foam furniture. If covers cannot be removed, have them professionally cleaned or clean with an upholstery shampoo and spotting kit – test on hidden areas first. Do not over-wet. Dry-clean chenilles, tapestries, velours, velvets and fabrics containing silk, wool or viscose.
- **Care:** position upholstery away from sunlight to avoid fading. Clean before it becomes heavily soiled.
- **To remove pet hairs:** if your vacuum cleaner does not successfully remove pet hairs from upholstery, pick them up by dabbing them with adhesive tape wrapped around your hand. For larger areas, put on a rubber glove, immerse your

gloved hand in water and wipe down the sofa or chair, taking care not to over-wet it. Rinse glove under tap to remove hairs.

Waxed jackets

Some brands can be cleaned by specialist companies, who will clean and re-wax jackets, trousers, hoods and waistcoats. Barbour jackets can be re-waxed, repaired and re-proofed by the manufacturer, J. Barbour; they do not recommend dry-cleaning. You can also re-wax any wear patches yourself using Nikwax or Grangers Superphy pump spray.

Wedding dresses
(including veils and christening gowns)

Always have professionally dry-cleaned before storing even if gown is not visibly dirty – colourless stains such as perfume can develop and discolour as they react with the air and these stains cannot be removed. Contact the Dry Cleaning Information Bureau for specialist dry-cleaners in your area.

- **Storage:** use a special acid-reduced cardboard box, and interleave dress with acid-free tissue, both available from Conservation by Design and Safe Storage Company Ltd. Do not use an ordinary cardboard box, plastic bags or PVC zip covers as chemicals from these packaging materials can leach through the tissue. Place box in a cool cupboard, away from damp, direct or indirect heat or sunlight. Inspect every 18 months to two years, refolding dress along slightly different lines to help prevent permanent creasing.
- **Vacuum packing:** professional vacuum packing should preserve gown for at least 25 years, but you won't be able to remove the dress as once the seal is broken the preserving properties will be lost. Available at Jeeves of Belgravia.

Removing stains and marks

IN THIS CHAPTER YOU WILL FIND

Here are the best ways to remove stains and marks from fabrics, upholstery, carpets, wooden surfaces and walls – and the best products to use.

THE 10 GOLDEN RULES OF STAIN REMOVAL

1. Always **act quickly** to remove stains. Blot up excess liquid using absorbent paper. Scrape off excess solids with a blunt knife.
2. Never **try to spot-clean** any stain with warm or hot water.
3. Never use water to sponge **oil-based stains** such as mayonnaise and curry sauce – it will set the stain.
4. Before treating a stain, **test remover** on a seam or hidden area. Take care with silk because some dyes are not colourfast and could watermark.
5. Read stain removal product **instructions** thoroughly and wear rubber gloves if you have sensitive skin.
6. Place a clean absorbent cloth over the stain and treat from the underside. Work from the **outside to the middle** of the stain, to avoid spreading it.
7. **Dab** rather than rub, which could damage fabric.
8. Small **repeated applications** work better than saturating the stain.
9. After treating, washable fabrics should be **machine-washed** using as high a temperature as the fabric will allow. Wash dark coloured items separately.
10. Dry-clean-only fabrics should be **professionally cleaned**.

Adhesives

Quickly scrape off any excess. Follow stain removal information on packaging, or contact adhesive manufacturer.

ALL-PURPOSE HOUSEHOLD ADHESIVES

- **Carpets and fabrics:** dab area with acetone until glue has dissolved. Launder where possible.

▶

CONTACT ADHESIVES (EG EVO-STIK)

These harden on contact, so work quickly. Treat as all-purpose adhesives.

EPOXY RESIN (EG ARALDITE)

These consist of two parts, a glue and a hardener. Once hardened, they are almost impossible to remove. Use acetone or methylated spirits to remove any residue before they set.

- **Carpets and fabrics:** dab with cellulose thinners or methylated spirits. Once dry, glue can be removed only by cutting away the pile.

PAPER ADHESIVES (EG PRITT, COPYDEX) AND LATEX

- **Carpets:** pick off any residue before treating. Dab the stain with a dilute detergent solution, avoiding over-wetting. Rinse and dab dry.
- **Fabrics:** remove as much residue as possible. Dried adhesive will wash out. If any greasy marks remain, treat with an appropriate stain remover.

SUPER GLUES (EG LOCTITE)

- **Carpets:** sponge area with warm, soapy water to dissolve glue – you may have to do this several times. Be careful not to over-wet carpet, and blot afterwards to remove excess water. If this doesn't work, try a glue remover such as Loctite Glue Remover, a gel available from DIY stores. Test hidden area of carpet for colourfastness first.
- **Fabrics:** dab with acetone or use a proprietary glue remover.
- **Skin:** use special glue remover made by the manufacturer, or immerse in hot, soapy water to soften.

Alcohol spots, heat marks and water marks

See Fixing Things, p.216.

Animal stains

- **Carpets:** scrape away or blot up excess carefully. Flush area with a solution of sodium bicarbonate, or sponge with warm water. Blot dry. Clean and deodorise area with a proprietary pet stain remover such as X=O brand products or Help!. Shampoo carpet if necessary and blot dry.
- **Fabrics and upholstery:** scrape away any deposit and blot dry. If it is not possible to remove the area, isolate and gather it up by tying string tightly around it. Rinse under cold running water or treat with a proprietary pet stain remover such as those made by Shaws, available from pet shops.

Artists' paints

ACRYLIC

If still wet, blot excess paint with absorbent paper and wash out with soap and water. If stain has dried, place an absorbent pad under it, if possible, and dab with cotton-wool moistened with a liquid stain remover or methylated spirits. On synthetics, test area first.

OIL

Almost impossible to remove, but try holding an absorbent pad under stain, dabbing right side with white spirit. Sponge or wash as normal.

▶

POSTER, POWDER AND WATERCOLOUR
Sponge well with cold water, or soak in cold water if necessary. Wash as normal. Remove remaining traces with methylated spirits.

Ballpoint pen

SEE ALSO

Tried and tested products, Fabric Stains, p.212

■ **Fabrics and upholstery:** dab gently with cotton wool moistened with a solution of hydrogen peroxide, available from chemists (one part 20-vol peroxide to six parts cold water) – but do not use on nylon and do not soak for more than 30 minutes. Machine-wash if possible. If unsuccessful, contact the manufacturer for advice, or dry-clean.

■ **Suede:** rub gently with abrasive paper or a suede-cleaning block. Alternatively, seek professional advice.

■ **Vinyl upholstery, wallcoverings and bags:** must be treated immediately or cannot be removed. Scrub with warm detergent solution, using an old nailbrush.

Beer

■ **Carpets:** clean with proprietary carpet shampoo or carpet spotting kit available from department stores. Alternatively, try a proprietary carpet stain remover, followed by a carpet shampoo. On old stains, try dabbing with methylated spirits.

■ **Upholstery and non-washable fabrics:** blot and wipe with warm water. Remove dried stains with a white vinegar solution (one part vinegar to five parts water), then with clear water. Blot to dry.

■ **Washable fabrics:** machine-wash with a biological detergent. Soak dried stains in a warm washing soda or a proprietary pre-wash detergent solution such as Vanish Pre-Wash. Wash as normal using as hot a wash as possible.

Beetroot

- **Table linen**: sponge immediately with cold water and soak in cold water overnight if possible. Then wash using a biological detergent. For stubborn and dried stains, try a proprietary fruit and wine stain remover such as Stain Devils No.6.

Bird droppings

- **Canvas and awnings:** allow to dry thoroughly then brush off with a stiff brush. If marks remain, dip brush in a biological detergent solution and rub area. Hose down and rinse well.
- **Washing on the line:** scrape off deposit, then wash items again as normal. If stains persist on white or colourfast fabrics (not polyamide/nylon) immerse complete items in a solution of hydrogen peroxide, available at chemists (one part 20-vol peroxide to six parts cold water) – but do not soak for more than 30 minutes. Wash and rinse thoroughly.

Blackcurrant juice

SEE *ALSO*

For recommended products, see Fabric Stains, p.212

- **Carpets:** blot up as much as possible while still wet, using absorbent paper. Rub with a stain-removing bar and shampoo area.
- **Fabrics:** rinse under cold water. Pre-soak in a solution of washing soda, then machine-wash at as hot a temperature as fabric allows using a biological detergent. Treat dried stains with a proprietary fruit and wine stain remover such as Stain Devils No. 6 before washing. If stubborn stains persist on non-nylon whites, try bleaching with dilute household bleach. Rinse thoroughly.

■ **Upholstery:** sponge with cold water and blot dry. Dab dark, dried stains with a solution of hydrogen peroxide, available at chemists (one part 20-vol peroxide to six parts water) – but do not use on nylon and do not leave wet for more than 30 minutes.

Blood

■ **Bedding and washable fabrics:** sponge with cold water. Machine-wash using a biological detergent and a wash temperature as high as fabric allows. Pre-soak dried stains using a pre-wash detergent or washing soda. Wash as above.

■ **Carpets:** dab with kitchen towel as soon as possible, then sponge with cold water and blot dry. If stain remains, use a specialist carpet stain remover. Dried stains may need professional treatment – contact the National Carpet Cleaners' Association for advice.

■ **Mattresses:** dried stains are difficult to remove. Tip mattress on its side and sponge with cold water. Blot thoroughly. Treat with a foam carpet or upholstery shampoo. Rinse and blot dry.

■ **Non-washable fabrics and upholstery:** brush away surface deposit and sponge with cold water. Rinse and blot dry. For stubborn stains use the foam from an upholstery shampoo or have professionally cleaned.

Candle wax

■ **Carpets:** make sure wax is really hard before trying to remove it by filling a plastic bag with ice cubes and placing it over the area. Scrape off the excess candle wax deposit, then remove remainder by placing a sheet of absorbent kitchen paper over the area and ironing gently. Do not let iron touch the carpet pile or it may scorch and melt. Keep moving the paper around for maximum absorption, and continue until all the wax has been absorbed. Remove any remaining colour or stain with methylated spirits (test first on an inconspicuous area as it may discolour carpet) or use a proprietary carpet stain remover.

- **Table linen and washable fabrics:** scrape away surface deposit using the back edge of a blunt knife. Place clean absorbent paper on both sides of stain and melt out remaining wax using a warm iron. Launder the item as normal, using a hot wash if possible.
- **Upholstery:** melt out using a moderately hot iron and white absorbent paper. Remove any remaining colour by dabbing with methylated spirits. On pile fabrics, try removing the deposit by rubbing lightly with a cloth, or melt it out by placing absorbent paper on carpet pile and, if possible, ironing the reverse side.
- **Wooden surfaces:** chip away at the wax when hard, using your fingernail or a plastic spatula. Remove remaining film with a duster, and polish as normal. If heat marking has occurred, rub along grain with a metal polish.

Chewing gum

SEE ALSO

For recommended products, see Carpet Stains, p.210 and Fabric Stains, p.212

The best way to remove chewing gum stuck onto fabric is to place the fabric in the freezer, or alternatively hold a plastic bag of ice cubes on the area to harden the gum. Once the gum is completely brittle try to pick it off, or, if that doesn't work, try scraping it off using a blunt knife.

Chocolate and cocoa

SEE *ALSO*

For recommended products, see Carpet Stains, p.210

- **Carpets:** blot or scrape up any excess deposit using a blunt knife. Treat stained area with carpet shampoo or a carpet spotting kit. Treat any remaining stain with a proprietary stain remover, then shampoo carpet as normal.
- **Fabrics:** scrape off excess deposit using the back of a knife blade. Soak in a solution of washing soda or proprietary pre-wash detergent such as Vanish Pre-Wash, then machine wash items at as high a temperature as the fabric allows, using a biological detergent.
- **Upholstery:** blot or scrape up any deposit with the back of a knife. Use a proprietary carpet stain remover, rinse and blot gently to dry.

Coffee

SEE *ALSO*

For recommended products, see Carpet Stains, p.210 and Fabric Stains, p.212; Ring Marks, p.222

- **Carpets:** flush fresh stains with cold water and blot well to dry. Treat dried stains with a carpet shampoo.
- **Fabrics:** soak in a warm solution of washing soda or pre-wash detergent, then wash at as high a temperature as the fabric allows using a biological detergent.
- **Upholstery:** sponge with cold water, treat with carpet stain remover, then shampoo.

Correction fluid

- **Carpets and upholstery:** allow to dry and pick off as much of the deposit as possible, taking care not to snag fabric. Treating with turpentine will fade but not remove mark. Remainder can only be cleaned by professional treatment.
- **Fabrics:** try acetone or turpentine followed by repeated washing, but professional treatment is recommended.

Crayon

■ **Vinyl wallcoverings and bedheads:** wipe with a damp cloth. If necessary, use a proprietary stain remover.

■ **Wallpaper and painted walls:** impossible to remove. Repaint or patch in section of wallpaper.

Curry

SEE ALSO

For recommended products, see Carpet Stains, p.210 and Fabric Stains, p.212; see also Food Mixers and Processors, p.143

■ **Carpets:** act quickly. Treat small areas with carpet stain remover, then shampoo. Large stains should be professionally cleaned.

■ **Fabrics:** sponge fresh stains with a detergent solution before and after dabbing with an all-purpose stain remover, then machine wash. Treat dried stains on white and colourfast fabrics (except nylon) with a solution of hydrogen peroxide, available from chemists (one part 20-vol peroxide to six parts water), then machine-wash. Heavy stains may not come out. Dry-clean non-washable fabrics.

■ **Upholstery:** have professionally treated.

Dyes

■ **Carpets, upholstery and non-washable fabrics:** it is best to have these professionally treated.

■ **Washable fabrics:** soak in a cold-water solution of washing soda or proprietary pre-wash detergent to avoid setting dye. Machine-wash using a biological detergent. On whites, try a proprietary colour-run remover such as Dylon, which can be used in a washing machine on a 60°C wash, making soaking unnecessary. Alternatively, soak in a weak bleach solution. Rinse thoroughly.

Egg

- **Carpets:** scrape to remove as much deposit as possible. Treat with proprietary carpet shampoo.
- **Fabrics:** rinse through with cold water. Soak and wash using a biological detergent.
- **Upholstery:** scrape off surface deposit and sponge with cold water, then clean water. Blot dry. Treat with an upholstery shampoo such as Bissell.

Fats, grease and oils

SEE ALSO

For recommended products, see Carpet Stains, p.211 and Fabric Stains, p.213

- **Carpets:** place some blotting or kitchen paper on stain and iron with a cool iron. Treat with a proprietary shampoo.
- **Fabrics:** wash cotton at 40°C with a biological detergent to remove stain. If the stain is heavy, pre-treat it with a proprietary stain remover such as Biotex. On wool or silk fabrics, use recommended stain removers.
- **Upholstery:** sprinkle talc on stain or blot with kitchen towel. Leave for several hours, then brush off. If marks remain after this, try an all-purpose stain remover. Sponge with water and blot dry.

Felt-tip pen

SEE ALSO

For recommended products, see Carpet Stains, pp.210–211 and Fabric Stains, p.212

- **Carpets:** before it dries, blot with absorbent paper, then use a carpet shampoo.
- **Fabrics and upholstery:** while still wet, blot up as much as possible with absorbent paper. Wash cotton fabrics at 40°C.

Fizzy drinks

SEE ALSO

For recommended products, see Carpet Stains, pp.210–211

■ **Carpets:** blot away as much as you can while still wet then use a carpet shampoo.

Foundation cream

SEE ALSO

For recommended products, see Fabric Stains, p.212

■ **Fabrics:** clear away any surface deposit. Soak using a pre-wash detergent, then machine-wash at as high a temperature as the fabric will allow with a biological powder. Remove light markings with a proprietary grease and oil stain remover such as Stain Slayer. For stubborn stains, wash in a detergent solution, treat with an all-purpose stain remover and re-wash. Dry-clean the item if not machine washable.

■ **Upholstery:** wipe away wet deposits or brush away dried stains. Sponge with a detergent solution and treat with an all-purpose stain remover. Sponge again with detergent solution, then rinse with clean water. Blot well to dry.

Glues

See Adhesives, p.185.

Grass

SEE ALSO

For recommended products, see Fabric Stains, p.212

■ **Fabrics:** treat with proprietary grass stain remover such as Stain Devils No.5, then machine-wash using a biological detergent. Use as high a temperature as possible. Dry-clean non-washable fabrics.

Gravy

- **Fabrics:** pre-wash or soak using a proprietary product such as Vanish Pre-Wash, then machine-wash using a biological detergent. Use a hot wash if possible.
- **Upholstery:** treat as for foundation cream (see p.197).

Grease

See Fats, Grease and Oils, p.196

Ice cream

- **Carpets:** scrape away deposit and wipe up as much excess as possible. Shampoo area. Treat any remaining stains with a carpet shampoo.
- **Fabrics:** soak, then wash in a biological detergent using as hot a wash as possible.
- **Upholstery:** sponge with warm water, then treat with a solution of hydrogen peroxide, available at chemists (one part 20-vol peroxide to six parts cold water) – but do not use on nylon and do not soak for more than 30 minutes. Rinse and blot dry.

Ink

- **Carpets:** contact ink manufacturer for advice. Tackle immediately. Remove as much as possible by dabbing with absorbent paper or a dry cloth. When you have soaked up as much as you can, wet the stain with water, soda water or a bicarbonate of soda solution (1 tsp to 0.5 litre/1 pint water) and continue to blot with a pad of clean paper or cloth. Do not use washing-up liquid or detergent until all the ink has been removed as it will 'set' the stain. If stains remain, try a carpet spotting kit or have professionally treated.

- **Fabrics:** act quickly. On fresh spills dab the mark with a clean cloth soaked in milk, then launder. Alternatively, sponge or hold under cold running water until excess ink is removed. Machine-wash if possible using a high temperature and biological detergent. If staining remains, rub area with lemon juice and rinse thoroughly. Keep repeating until clear. Alternatively, soak in a solution of hydrogen peroxide, available at chemists (one part 20-vol peroxide to six parts cold water) – but do not use on nylon and do not soak for more than 30 minutes, then launder. Treat dried stains on white cotton and linen with a dilute solution of household bleach. For other whites and coloureds, try a proprietary ink remover such as Stain Devils No.1 or No. 4. Dry-clean non-washable fabrics.
- **Upholstery:** treat with an upholstery spotting kit or upholstery shampoo. Avoid over-wetting.

Iron mould

- **Fabrics:** rub with lemon juice, cover with salt and leave for at least an hour. Rinse and wash items as normal. Treat any particularly stubborn stains with a proprietary stain remover such as Stain Devils No. 7.

Ketchup and bottled sauces

SEE ALSO

For recommended products, see Fabric Stains, p.213

- **Carpets:** carefully remove excess with the back edge of a knife, taking care not to spread the stain further; soften dried stains by blotting with a solution of glycerine, available at chemists (equal parts glycerine and water). Then blot gently with soda water or a baking soda solution (1 tsp bicarbonate of soda to 0.5 litre/1 pint water). When the stain has been removed, apply foam from a carpet shampoo ▶

or spray, working from the outside inwards – do not use shampoo any earlier as it will 'set' the stain. Rinse the area and dry well.

- **Fabrics:** pre-soak, then wash with a biological detergent.
- **Upholstery:** sponge with cold water followed by a detergent solution. Avoid over-wetting. Rinse well and blot dry. If marks persist, use an all-purpose stain remover, then rinse.

Lipstick

SEE ALSO

For recommended products, see Fabric Stains, p.213

- **Carpets:** scrape away any deposit, treat with a proprietary grease and oil stain remover, then shampoo.
- **Fabrics:** soak in a detergent solution, then dab with an all-purpose stain remover such as Stain Devils No. 5. Wash off with a detergent solution then launder. Lipstick is difficult to remove from natural fabrics.
- **Upholstery:** have professionally treated.

Mayonnaise

- **Fabrics:** sponge with warm water – not hot water, which will set stain. Soak and wash in a biological detergent.
- **Upholstery:** remove excess, taking care not to spread stain. Treat with proprietary grease and oil stain remover. Rinse and blot dry.

Mildew

- **Fabrics:** normal washing should remove fresh mildew marking. Treat old stains on white fabric (except nylon) with a bleach solution – either 20-vol hydrogen peroxide (available from chemists) or household bleach (20ml/¾fl oz bleach for every 5 litres/9 pints water). Treat white and colourfast fabrics, except acetates, with a stain remover such as Stain Devils No. 7. Wash regularly to reduce marks.

SEE ALSO
Bathroom cleaning,
pp.111–114

- **Plastic shower curtains:** sponge marks with a bleach solution, diluted as above. Rinse thoroughly, then treat the curtains with a fungicide.
- **Upholstery:** brush away spores and spray with a proprietary fungicide such as Mystox to kill bacteria. Dab marks with a mild disinfectant until removed, then sponge with cold water to rinse. Mattresses can also be treated with mild disinfectant – start with a dilute solution, then get more concentrated until mildew is cleared. Consult the Victoria & Albert Museum for advice on treating items of value.
- **Walls:** strip off wallpaper (if necessary), wash down with a mild detergent solution, then wipe over with a mould killer or inhibitor such as Cuprinol.

Milk

- **Carpets:** treat quickly. Flush area with warm water and blot to dry, then use a carpet stain remover. Neutralise lingering smells with a proprietary deodoriser such as Neutradol.
- **Fabrics:** rinse in lukewarm water, then wash as normal. Soak dried stains first in a biological detergent solution.
- **Upholstery:** sponge with lukewarm water and blot dry, then use a suitable stain remover.

Mould

See Mildew, p.200. For iron mould, see Rust, p.204.

Mud

- **Carpets:** leave to dry, then brush and vacuum. Use a carpet spot cleaner or shampoo to remove marks.
- **Fabrics:** soak in cold water, then machine-wash with a biological detergent.
- **Upholstery:** lightly brush when mud is completely dry. Sponge remaining marks with a warm, mild detergent solution. Sponge with clear water to rinse, and blot dry.

Mystery stains

- **Fabrics:** wash as normal, adding an in-wash stain remover for an extra boost. For delicates, use a little detergent dissolved in cool water and gently rub the stained section, fabric to fabric, then wash as normal. For stains on white washable fabric (except nylon), try soaking in a solution of household bleach (20ml/¾fl oz bleach to 5 litres/9 pints water).
- **If dry-cleaning has 'set' the stain:** as a last resort, try treating stain with an in-wash stain remover, followed by machine-washing on a 40°C wash cycle with biological detergent. Bear in mind, though, that the garment may fade and shrink if you do this.

Nail varnish

- **Carpets:** treat with a carpet shampoo. Have any remaining marks professionally cleaned.
- **Fabrics:** a real problem. Dabbing with nail varnish remover that contains acetone will fade the mark but is unlikely to remove it totally. Dry-cleaning may be effective.
- **Upholstery:** have professionally treated.

Paints

SEE ALSO
Artists' paints, p.189

OIL-BASED
Dabbing with white spirit may help fade marks, but they are usually permanent. Professional cleaning may help.

WATER-BASED
Rinse out or flush fresh marks with cold water, then launder. Dried marks are difficult to remove, but treating with a proprietary paint remover may fade them.

Perfume

- **Non-washable fabrics:** lubricate with a solution of glycerine, available at chemists (equal parts glycerine and water), leave for up to an hour then sponge clean, avoiding over-wetting. Blot dry. It is best to dry-clean expensive items and silk as they may watermark.
- **Washable fabrics:** rinse through immediately. Lubricate dried stains as above or use a proprietary fruit and wine stain remover such as Stain Devils No.6 before washing as normal.

Perspiration

See Sweat, p.207.

Pollen

SEE ALSO
For recommended products, see Carpet Stains, p.211 and Fabric Stains, p.213

- **Carpets:** gently lift away from fabric using sticky tape, then use a proprietary stain remover.
- **Fabrics:** try dabbing fresh pollen stains with adhesive tape or use vacuum nozzle on low suction. Treat stains with proprietary grass stain remover such as Stain Devils No.5 or Dylon Fabric Care. Wash as normal.

Red wine

SEE ALSO

For recommended products, see Carpet Stains, p.211 and Fabric Stains, p.213

Act quickly. Sponge area clean with sparkling or soda water before blotting dry with kitchen paper. Alternatively, use Wine Away, which turns the stain blue, then removes it when sponged or laundered.

■ **Carpets:** sponge with sparkling water and blot dry. Treat with a carpet shampoo and rinse well. If stains persist, try a carpet spotting kit, then shampoo. Never use salt as this will set the stain.

■ **Fabrics:** sponge fresh stains with sparkling water, then follow with normal laundering. Treat dried stains with a proprietary stain remover or a solution of hydrogen peroxide, available at chemists (one part 20-vol peroxide to six parts cold water) – but do not use on nylon and do not soak for more than 30 minutes – then wash as normal.

■ **Upholstery:** sponge with warm water and blot well. Treat with an upholstery shampoo.

Rust

■ **Carpets:** use a solution of warm water and biological washing powder or liquid (10 parts water to one part detergent), testing first on a small hidden area. If the stain does not come out, try a stronger solution, but you should avoid over-wetting the carpet.

■ **Fabrics:** rust stains on clothes that have been through the washing machine are likely to be ironmould – a mould that develops if a rusty mark is left untreated. If your washing machine is old, this may be responsible, so check for any rust marks before and after clothes go into the wash. Wash as normal to remove light rust marks. Treat heavily marked areas with a proprietary rust and iron mould remover such as Stain Devils No. 7. Ironmould is easily transferred from

one garment to another, so be vigilant and treat affected
clothes as soon as possible.

Salt and water marks

- **Fabrics:** remove watermarks from viscose by wetting the whole garment to give a uniform finish. This is also worth trying on non-washable silk if the dry-cleaner can't help and you've nothing to lose.
- **Leather or suede fabrics:** let the item dry out naturally at normal room temperature in a well-ventilated room. Brush out marks on suede using a suede brush to even out the colour. On leather, use a proprietary product such as Dasco Clean and Care aerosol.
- **Leather and suede shoes:** moisten stain and rub with a soft cloth, or try a proprietary product – Kiwi have a range. After treating, spray shoes with a water-repellent spray protector.
- **Nubuck:** use special nubuck cleaner such as Dasco Suede and Nubuck Cleaner or Kiwi Select Nubuck Cleaner. Do not use suede cleaners or brushes as they will flatten pile.

Scorch marks

- **Carpets:** for light marks, trim tufts with scissors to remove damaged area. If scorching is heavier, remove any loosened fibres with a stiff-bristled brush, then make gentle circular movements with a piece of glasspaper to hide the area. Contact the British Carpet Manufacturers' Association for companies who will re-tuft or patch a small area.
- **Fabrics:** impossible to remove heavily scorched marks, but you may be able to fade light marks by washing as usual, adding a liquid in-wash stain remover, such as Vanish, or

▶

soaking in a solution of 15ml (1 tbsp) washing soda to 500ml (¾ pint) warm water for a couple of hours before normal washing.

Shoe polish

- **Carpets:** carefully scrape away excess, dab with proprietary carpet stain remover, then use a carpet shampoo to dissolve any polish residue.
- **Fabrics:** first scrape away deposit and treat them with a proprietary stain cleaner such as Stain Devils No. 5 before rinsing and laundering.
- **Upholstery:** scrape away deposit. Sponge with warm water, blot dry, then sponge with biological detergent, avoiding over-wetting and scuffing surface. Rinse and blot dry.

Soot

- **Carpets:** do not brush. Use the nozzle attachment of your vacuum cleaner to pick up soot residue. Try absorbing stain with talcum powder – rub in lightly, then vacuum away deposit. If stains still remain, try a proprietary carpet stain remover such as Spot Shot, followed by a carpet shampoo such as 1001 All Purpose and Carpet Cleaner.
- **Fabrics:** vacuum residue. Washing will gradually fade stain.

Soy sauce

- **Fabrics:** launder using a biological detergent.
- **Upholstery:** sponge with cold water, then with a biological detergent solution. Rinse and dry thoroughly.

Scorch marks

Sweat

- **Non-washable fabrics:** dry-clean heavily stained areas. On lightly soiled areas try a solution of white vinegar (15ml/1 tbsp vinegar to 250ml/⅓ pint warm water) to clean and deodorise area, but it may watermark.
- **Washable fabrics:** soak colourfast items overnight. Scrub affected areas with a nailbrush, then wash with a biological detergent, adding Vanish In-Wash Stain Remover to the wash. For stubborn stains, gently work in some of the stain remover or use a solution of half glycerine, half warm water and leave for an hour before washing.

Tar

- **Carpets:** scrape gently to remove deposit. Very hard marks may need softening first with a solution of glycerine, available at chemists (equal parts glycerine and warm water). Leave for up to an hour, rinse with clean water and blot well. Then use a proprietary cleaner such as Bissell.
- **Fabrics:** scrape carefully to remove as much surface deposit as possible. Hold an absorbent pad over stain and dab it from below with cotton-wool moistened with Olbas (eucalyptus) oil, available from chemists, or Swarfega hand cleanser (from DIY stores, garages and petrol stations). Or use a proprietary stain remover such as Stain Slayer.
- **Shoes (leather):** test first on instep, then try dabbing with a little white spirit.

▶

Tea

- **Carpets:** sponge with cold water. Treat with a carpet shampoo. Rinse and blot dry.
- **Fabrics:** rinse fresh stains in warm water, then wash as normal using a biological detergent. Loosen dried stains with a pre-wash treatment before machine washing.
- **Upholstery:** rinse with cold water, then apply a biological detergent solution. Rinse thoroughly and blot dry. Try a proprietary carpet stain remover such as Vanish or 1001 on stubborn stains, but do not leave on for too long.
- **Wooden surfaces:** to remove stains caused by dripping tea-bags, rub neat washing-up liquid gently into the stains with a green scourer. Rinse, then dry.

Urine

SEE ALSO

Fabric Deodorisers, p.180

- **Carpets:** flush area with cold water and blot until nearly dry. Sponge with a carpet shampoo solution. Rinse well with cold water to which a few drops of disinfectant have been added. Blot to dry. If odour persists, try a deodorising product such as Febreze or Neutradol.
- **Mattresses:** hold the mattress on its side and sponge with a cold solution of washing-up liquid or upholstery shampoo. Wipe with cold water to which a few drops of disinfectant have been added. Alternatively, use the foam from carpet shampoo to clean the mattress.
- **Non-washable fabrics:** remove fresh stains by sponging with a vinegar solution (15ml/1 tbsp vinegar to 500ml/¾ pint warm water). Dried stains should be professionally treated.
- **Washable fabrics:** rinse, then soak overnight in a biological detergent solution. Machine-wash as normal.

Vomit

SEE ALSO
Fabric Deodorisers,
p.180

- **Carpets:** scoop up as much as possible and clean with a bicarbonate of soda solution. Blot well. Rub in a foam carpet shampoo solution, repeating until stain has cleared. Rinse with warm water to which a few drops of antiseptic have been added. Blot well. If odour persists, try a deodorising product such as Febreze or Neutradol.
- **Fabrics:** remove any deposit and rinse well with cold water. Machine-wash using a biological detergent if possible. Dry-clean expensive or non-washable fabrics. If odour persists, try a fabric deodoriser such as Neutradol.
- **Upholstery:** scoop up surface deposit and sponge area with warm water. Blot dry. Try an upholstery cleaner such as Vanish or 1001, or foam from a carpet shampoo. If odour persists, try a fabric deodoriser.

CARPET STAINS: TRIED AND TESTED PRODUCTS

STAIN	TREATMENT TO TRY FIRST	WOOL-MIX CARPET	NYLON CARPET
Chewing gum	Hold a plastic bag of ice cubes on the gum until it is brittle enough to pick off	De.Solv.It Spot Shot 1001 Mousse for Carpet & Upholstery Vanish Carpet and Upholstery Mousse	De.Solv.It Spot Shot 1001 Mousse for Carpet & Upholstery Vanish Carpet and Upholstery Mousse
Chocolate		Bissell Carpet Cleaner Scotchguard Cleaner for Rugs and Carpets Spot Shot White Wizard Woolite Handwash solution Fairy Liquid solution	Bissell Carpet Cleaner Scotchguard Cleaner for Rugs and Carpets Spot Shot White Wizard Woolite Handwash solution Fairy Liquid solution
Coffee	Dilute area with cold water, then blot	1001 Mousse for Carpet & Upholstery Spot Shot White Wizard Vanish Carpet and Upholstery Mousse Woolite Handwash solution Fairy Liquid solution	1001 Mousse for Carpet & Upholstery Scotchgard Cleaner for Rugs and Carpets Spot Shot White Wizard Woolite Handwash solution
Curry		1001 Mousse for Carpet & Upholstery and Vanish Mousse both faded stains after several applications, but no product totally removed curry marks	1001 Mousse for Carpet & Upholstery and Vanish Mousse both faded stains after several applications, but no product totally removed curry marks
Felt-tip pen	Before it dries, blot with absorbent paper	Bissell Carpet Cleaner 1001 Mousse for Carpet & Upholstery Spot Shot White Wizard Vanish Carpet and Upholstery Mousse Woolite Handwash solution Fairy Liquid solution	Bissell Carpet Cleaner 1001 Mousse for Carpet & Upholstery Scotchgard Cleaner for Rugs and Carpets Spot Shot White Wizard Vanish Carpet and Upholstery Mousse Fairy Liquid solution

CARPET STAINS: TRIED AND TESTED PRODUCTS

STAIN	TREATMENT TO TRY FIRST	WOOL-MIX CARPET	NYLON CARPET
Fizzy drinks	Blot away as much as you can while still wet	Bissell Carpet Cleaner 1001 Mousse for Carpet & Upholstery Spot Shot Vanish Carpet and Upholstery Mousse Woolite Handwash solution	1001 Mousse for Carpet & Upholstery Vanish Carpet and Upholstery Mousse Woolite Handwash solution
Grease	Blot away excess, then sprinkle with talc and vacuum area	1001 Mousse for Carpet & Upholstery Spot Shot White Wizard Vanish Carpet and Upholstery Mousse Woolite Handwash solution Fairy Liquid solution	Bissell Carpet Cleaner 1001 Mousse for Carpet & Upholstery Scotchgard Cleaner for Rugs and Carpets Spot Shot White Wizard Vanish Carpet and Upholstery Mousse Woolite Handwash solution Fairy Liquid solution
Pollen	Gently lift away from fabric using sticky tape, or vacuum up using the crevice nozzle	Woolite Handwash solution	White Wizard Woolite Handwash solution
Red wine	Pour sparkling water or white wine over the stain, then blot	Spot Shot Wine Away	1001 Mousse for Carpet & Upholstery Spot Shot White Wizard Vanish Carpet and Upholstery Mousse

▶

WASHABLE FABRICS: TRIED AND TESTED STAIN REMOVAL PRODUCTS

STAIN	COTTON FABRIC	SILK FABRIC	WOOL FABRIC
Ballpoint pen	No product worked	Stain Devils No. 1, but act quickly	Dylon Fabric Care Stain Remover 1 Stain Devils No. 1
Blackcurrant juice	40°C wash Dylon Fabric Care Stain Remover 2 Stain Devils No. 6 White Wizard	Stain Devils No. 6	Stain Devils No. 6, but act quickly
Chewing gum	40°C wash Betterware Sticky Stuff Remover De.Solv.It	Stain Devils No. 3 Dylon Fabric Care Stain Remover 2 Stain Devils No. 4	The Stain Slayer
Coffee	40°C wash De.Solv.It Dylon Fabric Care Stain Remover 2 White Wizard	Dylon Fabric Care Stain Remover 2 Stain Devils No. 4	De.Solv.It, but act quickly Dylon Fabric Care Stain Remover 2, but act quickly Stain Devils No. 4, but act quickly White Wizard, but act quickly
Curry	White Wizard, but act quickly	No product worked	No product worked
Felt-tip pen	40°C wash	No product worked	Dylon Fabric Care Stain Remover 1 (more effective on day-old stains)
Foundation cream	De.Solv.It, but act quickly	Stain Devils No. 5 (more effective on day-old stains)	Stain Devils No. 5 (more effective on day-old stains)
Grass	40°C wash White Wizard	White Wizard, but act quickly	De.Solv.It Stain Devils No. 5 White Wizard

WASHABLE FABRICS: TRIED AND TESTED STAIN REMOVAL PRODUCTS			
STAIN	COTTON FABRIC	SILK FABRIC	WOOL FABRIC
Grease	40°C wash with biological detergent Stain Devils No. 5 The Stain Slayer White Wizard	The Stain Slayer	Stain Devils No. 5 The Stain Slayer White Wizard
Ketchup	40°C wash, but act quickly White Wizard	Stain Devils No. 5	No product worked
Lipstick	40°C wash De.Solv.It Dylon Fabric Care Stain Remover 1 Stain Devils No. 5 The Stain Slayer White Wizard	Dylon Fabric Care Stain Remover 1, but act quickly	De.Solv.It Dylon Fabric Care Stain Remover 1
Mud	Stain Devils No. 5, but act quickly	No product worked	No product worked
Nail varnish	No product worked	No product worked	No product worked
Pollen	40°C wash Dylon Fabric Care Stain Remover 1 Stain Devils No. 5	Dylon Fabric Care Stain Remover 1 Stain Devils No. 5	40°C wash (more effective on day-old stains) De.Solv.It Dylon Fabric Care Stain Remover 1 Stain Devils No. 5
Red wine	40°C wash, but act quickly De.Solv.It Dylon Fabric Care Stain Remover 2	Dylon Fabric Care Stain Remover 2, but act quickly Stain Devils No. 6, but act quickly	No product worked
Rust	Stain Devils No. 7, but act quickly	Stain Devils No. 7, but act quickly	No product worked
Shoe polish	Stain Devils No. 5	No product worked	Stain Devils No. 5 (more effective on day-old stains)

PART 3

Problem solving

THIS PART OF THE book gives advice on how to deal
with common problems and emergencies you might
encounter in your home, from how to unblock a sink to
deciding when to call an ambulance. Whatever the
problem, you'll find a solution – whether it is something
you can deal with yourself or guidance on finding someone
who can help.

You'll even find invaluable information on how to make
a complaint about a product or service, including a sample
letter that you can copy.

Fixing things

IN THIS CHAPTER YOU WILL FIND

Here's how to repair fixtures and fittings around the home, from loose floorboards to a blocked drain, and where to go for professional help.

Baths and sinks

BLOCKAGES

SEE ALSO
Drains, p.220

SEE ALSO
Emergency repairs, p.249; How to make a home insurance claim, p.253

Partial blockage (water drains away slowly) try using a plunger to suck away blockage – cover overflow outlet with a cloth and add enough water to cover base of plunger before pumping it up and down. Alternatively, pour down a strong solution of washing soda (225g/8oz to 7 litres/12 pints boiling water). If neither approach works, try using curtain wire to fish out hair and solid waste from pipe.

Total blockage for sinks put a bowl or bucket underneath to catch dirty water, undo U-shaped trap beneath sink. Remove blockage with curtain wire or a wire coathanger.

CRACKED SEALANT

Gently scrape out existing sealant and make sure surfaces are clean and dry. Protect wall and bath, sink or basin with masking tape. Apply suitable new sealant into gap and press down with a wet spatula if necessary. Remove masking tape within five minutes and leave until completely dry – this will take about 24 hours.

TIP

Be prepared – make sure you know where to find your main stopcock in an emergency.

China

China Restoration
Helen Warren China
Restoration and
Oxford China
Restoration Studio,
Directory pp.271 and
272

Discontinued china
Chinamatch, China
Matching Service,
China Set and Match,
and Tablewhere,
Directory p.270 and
p.272

BREAKAGES

Even china that has broken into several pieces can be mended successfully using epoxy resin adhesive – though once repaired, china is best kept as an ornament, or for occasional use. Do not use a jug if you have mended the handle, and do not try to mend anything used to contain hot liquids. Precious or antique items should be repaired by an expert.

CHIPS

Do not repair chips in tableware. Hide chips in white china by mixing epoxy resin and artists' powder paint. When dry, coat with varnish to resemble glaze. Alternatively, try building up the level with thin layers of enamel paint, allowing each to dry before applying the next.

5 EASY STEPS TO PERFECT CHINA REPAIRS

1. Clean fragments with liquid detergent, to **remove all traces of grease** and dirt. Rinse and allow to dry completely.

2. Have a **trial run** at fitting the pieces together. Then number the pieces in pencil, in order of gluing.

3. Mix together the epoxy resin adhesive and hardener and **brush sparingly** along the broken edges of the two largest pieces. Press together. Wipe surface to remove excess adhesive. You can use a solvent such as methylated spirits or acetone, but avoid use on unglazed pottery.

4. **Hold china together** as it dries using elastic bands or masking tape, or by clamping it in a partly opened drawer. Ornaments and difficult shapes can be pressed into a piece of plasticine, or kept in place in a box of sand.

5. Glue and fix the other broken sections in place in the same way. Leave for **at least 24 hours** to harden completely.

PROBLEM SOLVING 219

Curtains

TEARS IN FABRIC

Light cottons, silks and synthetics bring edges of tear together as closely as possible without puckering fabric and sew neatly to a matching offcut of fabric to reinforce back of curtain – take this from a hem or seam if necessary, patching the hidden area with plain fabric.

Sheer, unlined fabrics make a seam along the tear. Re-hang and gather differently, if necessary, to hide repair.

Lace, nets and loosely woven fabrics remove a few strands from a hidden area, or buy thread as close in texture and colour to curtain material as possible. Weave carefully into damaged area, working from behind.

Doors

SQUEAKS

Oil ordinary hinges from time to time, to prevent sticking and squeaking – move door back and forth so oil is worked into hinge.

STICKING

Tighten hinges if screws have worked loose. If door still sticks, rub edges liberally with chalk. Open and close door several times – the problem spot will be where chalk rubs away the most. Rub problem areas with a candle to lubricate. If this fails, sand or plane door edge, leaving enough space to admit a knife blade all round – when using plane, work towards centre, where wood is strongest, to avoid damaging ▶

corners. If problem is at bottom of door, try opening and closing it over a piece of coarse sandpaper. Treat any bare wood – sand edge lightly, wipe with white spirit and repaint.

Drains

BLOCKAGES

If you have cleared the waste pipe of a sink or basin and the water still does not run away, if the toilet will not flush correctly or there is an unpleasant smell outside, your drains may be blocked. Sometimes a blockage forms when leaves and debris clog up an open gully at the base of a pipe – this is usually easy to clear by lifting the grate and cleaning it, or by fishing out solid waste with a stick or bent wire. Mesh covers to prevent the problem are available from DIY stores. If blockage is in underground pipes call in an expert such as Dyno-rod.

Electrical appliances

SCRATCHES

Touch up scratches on white appliances by wiping with white spirit and painting with white enamel, such as Hammerite, applied with an artists' brush. Proprietary products are also available. Use heat-resistant enamel for cookers and boilers.

Floors

LOOSE AND SQUEAKING FLOORBOARDS

Usually caused by central heating, which makes timber dry out and shrink. Once gaps appear between floorboards, they may rub together and squeak. Nail down any loose boards using wood tacks.

PATCHING VINYL FLOORS

It is always worth keeping an offcut of vinyl used on a floor in case flooring is accidentally scorched or torn. Place piece of new flooring over damaged area and cut through both pieces with a sharp trimming knife, following outline of design if there is a tile motif or similar regular pattern. Lift and discard damaged section. Clean floor underneath thoroughly and allow to dry. Stick down new patch of flooring to fit, using double-sided heavy-duty adhesive tape for loose-lay floors. If floor has been stuck down, clean away old adhesive and stick patch in place with new adhesive. Scrub gently with detergent and a brush or very fine wire wool until new patch matches.

Furniture

SEE ALSO

If the table is valuable or French-polished, contact British Antique Furniture Restorers' Association, Directory p.273; see also Care and cleaning, Furniture, p.123

ALCOHOL SPOTS, HEAT MARKS AND WATER MARKS

If surface has roughened, try smoothing by rubbing with very fine steel wool dipped in liquid wax polish, working in the direction of the grain. Use this method with extreme care on veneered finishes. If the surface is not roughened, put a dab of cream metal polish on a cloth and rub the wood briskly in the direction of grain. Work in small sections at a time, wiping away cream at intervals to check progress. Finish by polishing the table lightly with wax polish.

BLISTERS IN VENEER

Can sometimes be flattened by covering with a cotton tea towel and ironing. Leave for two days to see if there is an improvement; if not, slit with a safety blade and glue flat.

BROKEN MOULDINGS

May need replacing if damage is extensive. It is often possible to have simple patterns copied by a timber merchant. ▶

BURNS
Can be cut away with a safety blade. Sand hollow with fine abrasive paper and if damage is extensive, repair with wood filler stained to the correct colour. Otherwise, build up layers of varnish. Consider professional repair for good furniture.

CRACKS
Can be filled with wood filler and epoxy resin glue. Sand level with surface when dry.

DENTS
Can be filled, or drawn out by heat if bare wood. Wrap a pad of cotton wool in a cotton tea towel and soak in boiling water. Wearing rubber gloves, wring out pad and press on dent for several minutes. The wood should swell and lift the dent. Heat and moisture will bleach the surface so sand and stain when dry.

LOOSE CASTORS
Try packing screw holes with slivers of wood coated with woodworking glue, or move castor so that it screws into an undamaged piece of wood.

LOOSE HINGES
Caused by screw holes growing too large. Unscrew the hinge and replace with thicker screws, or make holes smaller by packing with wall plugs before replacing the hinge with the original screws.

SCRATCHES AND RING MARKS
Try masking light scratches using a similar-coloured wax crayon or shoe polish. After applying, leave for a while

before buffing briskly. Alternatively, use a proprietary product testing the colour match in a hidden area first. Deep scratches will need wood filler, stained to match surround.

STICKING DRAWERS

Often the result of damp, which makes wood swell. Check runners first to see if they are broken or need replacing – if intact, chalk drawer edges, push drawer shut as far as possible, then tug open. The areas rubbed clean of chalk will show where it sticks. Sand or plane until drawer closes easily, and spray runners with furniture polish so drawer opens and closes smoothly. Check base of drawer to see if it has split or warped, and replace if necessary.

WOBBLY CHAIRS

Uneven legs can be levelled by cutting legs to the length of the shortest leg, or by building up the short leg to match the rest. Glue and screw the extra piece of leg in place so the chair is perfectly stable.

Radiators

SEE ALSO

For advice on hiring a plumber see p.21

BLEEDING A RADIATOR

If radiator is colder at the top than at the bottom, or if it drums loudly when warming up, you need to bleed it to remove air. (If you have a sealed system you will require a plumber.) To bleed radiator: Turn off pump and boiler. Find square-shaped bleed valve at top corner of radiator and insert key (supplied when central heating was installed – or available from DIY or hardware stores). Holding a jar or bowl underneath valve to catch any water, turn key cautiously anti-clockwise, abut 90º. (Do not turn more than this or water will flood out.) Air will hiss as it escapes; as soon as it stops, ▶

and water starts to spill out, turn key clockwise to close valve. Bleed radiators once or twice a year as air can cause corrosion.

Tiles

CRACKED

To replace a cracked ceramic tile set in the middle of a wall or worktop, drill into centre of tile using a power drill fitted with a masonry bit. (Wear safety glasses and gloves and fix sticky tape over the spot you want to drill, to stop drill skidding.) Repeat until you have drilled several holes, then carefully chip away sections of tile with a chisel and hammer, working outwards from centre. Protect bath or sink from flying tile shards by covering with towels. Chisel away old adhesive in gap and spread new adhesive on the back of replacement. Press into place and re-grout.

SHABBY

Give old tiles a facelift by painting them. Clean, then rub surface with medium wet-and-dry abrasive paper used wet. Wash and dry thoroughly. Apply an even coat of zinc chromate primer and, when dry, cover with an oil-based undercoat. Leave to dry for a couple of days, then apply two coats of oil-based eggshell paint or proprietary tile paint, such as International. Re-grout between tiles or create fresh lines using a grout pen.

Toilets

DRIPPING OVERFLOW

A faulty ball valve or float cannot control the flow of water from the tank to the lavatory cistern, so water will drip through the overflow pipe. To stop this temporarily, tie the float arm to a piece of wood laid across the top of the cistern – but you won't be able to flush lavatory while this is in place. For a permanent repair, you will need to get in a plumber (see p.21) to replace or repair the ball float.

Walls

SEE ALSO

Painting problem solver, p.226; wallpaper problem solver, p.227

HANGING HEAVY PICTURES OR MIRRORS

Picture hooks are unlikely to hold the weight of heavy mirrors and pictures. Instead, use glass plate hooks, available from DIY stores, which have to be screwed to the wall and frame itself. For wooden frames, a normal screw will be sufficient, but for mirror or metal frames a self-tapping screw will grip better. Screw glass plate hooks into frame, check wall and plaster are sound, fit Rawlplugs and then screw to the wall.

Windows

LEAKS

If the window-sill is wood, it should have a drip groove underneath so that rain-water runs off, away from the house. If this is missing, paint or stain a fillet of wood to match the sill and nail it to the underside of the sill, near the front, to keep water away from the wall.

PAINTING PROBLEM SOLVER

PROBLEM	CAUSED BY	REMEDY
Blisters (raised bumps)	Painting damp wood	Allow paint to harden, then prick blister. If it is wet inside, you will need to strip back and fill grain before repainting
Cratering (depressions)	Too much damp in the atmosphere	Sand and repaint, keeping room warm and dry
Crazing (fine network of cracks)	Applying a second coat before first coat is dry	Allow to dry, then rub down and repaint
Flaking (flakes of paint coming away from wall)	Powdery or dirty walls underneath the new coat, or gloss paint that has not been sanded	Emulsion paint often flakes off woodwork and radiators, so rub it down and repaint with a coat of solvent-based eggshell or gloss
Runs (dribbles of paint)	Overloading brush	If only one or two, allow paint to dry completely then prick, rub down and touch in with a small paintbrush. Otherwise sand and start again
Specks and stray bristles (small lumps and bristles in paintwork)	Dirty wall or paint, or poor-quality brushes	Either sand down and start again or, in a small area, sand or pick out the pieces, rub with wet abrasive paper and touch in. This also works for insects trapped in wet paint

WALLPAPER PROBLEM SOLVER

PROBLEM	CAUSED BY	REMEDY
Bubbles	Wallpaper not pasted thoroughly or not given enough time to soak. Can also occur if length is not smoothed out properly	It is sometimes possible to slit air bubbles with a razor blade and paste edges into place
Dirty marks		Can usually be removed with a white eraser if used with care, or a piece of stale white bread
Peeling	Often caused by damp	If it is not substantial, try lifting and re-pasting edges with wallpaper paste or paper glue

Getting rid of things

IN THIS CHAPTER YOU WILL FIND

This chapter deals with the safe disposal of household items, and tells you what to do about nuisance calls, junk mail and noisy neighbours.

Items you no longer need

CAR BATTERIES, ENGINE OIL AND PETROL, DE-ICING FLUID
Dispose of safely at your local council waste disposal site.

COOKING OILS (USED)
Small amounts of used cooking oils can be soaked up with newspaper or kitchen towel, then thrown away with your normal rubbish, but take larger quantities in bottles along to your local council waste disposal site.

FRIDGES/FREEZERS
Since the beginning of 2002 it has become a legal requirement to remove ozone-depleting gases such as CFCs and HCFCs from fridges and freezers at the end of their life. Your local council can take away your old fridge, freezer or fridge/freezer, but there may be a fee. Alternatively, dispose of free of charge at your local council waste disposal site.

FURNITURE
Contact your local Council for Voluntary Service (your local library should have its number, or look on the National Association of Councils for Voluntary Service website), which will have details of charities in your area who could make use of unwanted furniture. Some local authorities run projects to ▶

provide furniture for new council tenants – like the charities, they may charge a small fee for collection.

Beds and sofas If these are pre-1988, the mattresses or stuffing probably won't be flame-retardant, so discard.

GARDEN WASTE
Take to your local council waste disposal site, or ring the council to arrange collection.

GAS CYLINDERS
Take back to where you bought them, or to a collection point at your local council waste disposal site.

INK AND TONER CARTRIDGES
Give spent cartridges from computer printers to a charity that can make money by recycling them, such as Scope and the Royal National Institute for the Blind.

MEDICINES AND TABLETS
Hand out-of-date medicines and tablets in to your local pharmacy, which will ensure they are disposed of safely.

MOBILE PHONES
Charities such as the British Red Cross and Oxfam accept mobile phones, batteries and chargers at their shops.

PAINT TINS
Leave the lid off emulsion and place in a well-ventilated room. Once it dries and solidifies throw tin in dustbin. Take gloss paint to the special collection area at local waste disposal site.

RECYCLING FACILITIES

Local councils organise regular collections of recyclable materials, such as newspapers and bottles, and will collect larger unwanted items on request. Alternatively, you may be able to use bottle and paper banks or drive your unwanted stuff to the tip. Find out what is available in your area by contacting the recycling officer at your local authority – the number will be listed in your local telephone directory.

Nuisances

JUNK MAIL/UNWANTED TELEPHONE SALES CALLS

To stop firms contacting you, register with a preference service. Advertisers will be given your details and told not to contact you, although this will not stop calls and mail from companies you have dealt with in the past, letters addressed to The Occupier, or mailings from abroad.

- **E-mails:** you can register to stop 'spam' – unsolicited E-mails – by logging on to www.e-mps.org.uk, the website of the E-mail Preference Service although some advertisers ignore this.
- **Faxes:** it is illegal to send sales and marketing faxes to an individual without their specific consent. If you are receiving them, register with the Fax Preference Service.
- **Letters:** the Mailing Preference Service covers all members of a household with the same surname. Re-register every five years.
- **Telephone calls and text messages:** the Telephone Preference Service covers fixed lines and mobiles, but cannot guarantee to stop unsolicited text messages. Registering is permanent and applies to the telephone number rather than the user.

▶

MALICIOUS PHONE CALLS

If you receive a malicious call, say nothing, walk away from
the phone and gently hang up without saying anything
after a few minutes – don't listen to hear if the caller is still
there. If the phone rings again, pick up the receiver but do
not speak – genuine callers will speak first. If the calls
continue, tell the operator, and keep a record of each call –
this may help the authorities trace the caller. BT can intercept
all your calls, and can change your number and make it
ex-directory. In serious cases, they work with the police to
trace the caller. For advice on dealing with malicious callers,
ring the free BT Malicious Calls Advice Line or the BT
Malicious Calls Bureau.

NOISY NEIGHBOURS

Start by approaching your neighbours about the problem –
explaining how the noise is affecting you or even asking
them to come and listen to it from your home. If they
are not helpful, contact your local council (ask for the
Environmental Health department), which has a duty to
investigate your complaint and to take legal action if it
decides a nuisance exists.

OVERHANGING TREES

If your neighbour's tree overhangs your garden, you are
entitled to ask them to trim it back. If they don't, you
have the right to trim it back to the boundary line. Your
neighbour owns any branches or fruit removed, so offer to
return them. Check with your local council before you do
any major surgery in case the tree in question is protected by
a preservation order.

STRAY CATS

To stop strays coming through your cat-flap, try fitting a cat-specific flap such as Cat Mate Electromagnetic Cat Flap, available from pet shops. This has two magnets – one in the cat-flap, the other on your cat's collar – to activate the lock.

Household pests

IN THIS CHAPTER YOU WILL FIND

Eradicating pests is simple if you know the best traditional remedies, pest control products, and where to go for professional help.

Ants

If you find more than a handful of ants, they could be nesting in your home. Check along skirting boards for the clue – tiny piles of earth. Although generally harmless, ants can be extremely unpleasant in large numbers. They appear between April and October, but the worst months are always July and August.

Treatment If practical, pour a kettle of boiling water over nest entrance, to kill the colony. Otherwise, use an insecticide – those carried back to the nest by ants, such as Nippon Ant Killer Liquid or Raid Ant Bait, are more effective than those that kill on contact. If the problem is unmanageable, your neighbours have ants too, or flying ants are swarming in your kitchen, contact the pest control division of your local authority's environmental health department or a pest control company who will deal with the problem for you.

Traditional remedies To repel ants: try sprinkling down cayenne pepper or cedar oil or plant strongly scented lavender, chives, spearmint and African marigolds by the back door, if that's where they are entering the house.

Bedbugs

Bites are usually the first sign; you may also be able to see the bugs, which are about the size of a match-head and brown, turning purple after they have bitten you. Infested rooms often have a slight almond odour. Bedbugs do not carry disease but bites can be irritating.

Treatment Contact the pest control division of your local authority's environmental health department.

Carpet beetles

Carpet beetles, also known as woollybears, are about 2–4mm long; they may be brown, black or mottled brown/grey/cream. If you spot them, act immediately as they will be looking for fabric such as carpets, clothing, blankets and fur in which to lay eggs. As the larvae hatch, they eat through their surroundings, leaving round holes. They can cause widespread, significant damage all year round.

Treatment Contact the pest control division of your local authority's environmental health department or your local pest control company.

Search loft for signs of birds' nests or feathers, often the source of carpet beetle infestation. Look for traces of damage in airing cupboards, wardrobes and chests where clothes are stored as well as under carpets and rugs.

Cockroaches

Usually appear in the evening, hiding during the day in pipes and behind sinks and stoves. Often confused with black

10 GOLDEN RULES OF PEST PREVENTION
1. Keep **food covered**, preferably in sealed containers or in the fridge.
2. Wrap rubbish well and dispose of it in sealed sacks and **animal-proof bins** if possible, well away from windows.
3. **Clean sink wastes** and drains regularly.
4. Stop up **cracks and holes**, especially around pipes.
5. Clean up **spills and crumbs** as soon as they occur.
6. **Vacuum** carpets, mattresses and upholstery frequently and move furniture regularly.
7. Clean up after **pets**.
8. Look behind and inside cupboards, lofts and sheds regularly so **pests cannot breed** undisturbed.
9. Turn out lofts, larders and other kitchen cupboards from time to time, to get rid of stale food and unwanted papers and textiles that pests may **feed on** or nest in.
10. Keep gutters and chimneys clear to prevent **birds nesting** and insects breeding.

beetles from the garden, they are identifiable by their long, whip-like antennae and flat, oval bodies. Cockroaches can easily find their way into cupboards in search of food.

Treatment Contact the pest control division of your local authority's environmental health department or your local pest control company – it is not easy to reach a nocturnal insect with insecticide.

Cockroaches cause food poisoning by contaminating food and preparation surfaces. Eradicate as quickly as possible.

Dustmites

A major factor in allergies such as rhinitis and allergic asthma, and thought to aggravate eczema. They cannot be eliminated from your home, however, because they are found in all textiles, especially pillows, mattresses and upholstery, where they live on flakes of human skin.

►

If affected Keep soft furnishings to a minimum, and look for fabrics, including bedding, that can be laundered at 60°C, which is hot enough to kill mites. If textiles are not washable, vacuum them regularly. Use a damp cloth when dusting, to keep airborne dust to a minimum. You can also buy sprays to eradicate mites, available from pharmacies – for details contact the National Asthma Campaign or Allergy UK.

Beds The older the bed, the more dustmites it is likely to contain. Consider investing in covers for pillows, mattresses and duvets made from microporous fabric that keeps house-mite debris in but still allows your body to breathe.

Fleas

Cat fleas are the most common, but human, bird and dog fleas will also bite. To check your pet for fleas, use a flea comb around its upper back, between the shoulders and up to the neck – look for a reddish-brown insect about 2mm long.

Treatment Fleas and their larvae can be all over the house, so you will need to treat both your pet and your home with separate products from the vet (not the pet shop) to kill them all. Household flea killer should be used on carpets, rugs, cracks in the floorboards, skirtings, upholstery and pet bedding – but not on human bedding. Your pet will need routine flea treatment every three months or so to prevent re-infestation. If treatment does not do the trick, contact the pest control division of your local authority's environmental health department or your local pest control company.

Flies

Houseflies spread food poisoning bacteria whenever they land on food or food preparation surfaces. If you have no control over the source of infestation, keep windows on the sunny side of the house closed or fit fly screens to them. Fly papers impregnated with insecticide can help. Reserve fly spray for individual flies, using sparingly and do not use over exposed food or fish tanks.

Traditional remedies To deter flies, you could try hanging bunches of mint or basil, or grow strongly-scented flowers such as marigolds and pelargoniums at doors or on window-sills.

CLUSTER FLIES
About the size of a housefly, these hibernate in roofs and attics and tend to return annually – signs of infestation are large quantities of lethargic and dead flies. Cluster flies can also be seen resting on south-facing walls.

Treatment Contact the pest control division of your local authority's environmental health department or a pest control company to help.

FRUIT FLIES
These tiny flies are attracted to rotting or over-ripe fruit and vegetables, and to fermenting liquids. Like all flies, they spread food poisoning bacteria when they land on your food. Fruit flies appear in September and October.

Treatment Check fruit bowls and vegetable racks, and throw away anything starting to rot. To kill flies of all kinds, use a suitable slow-release hanging unit.

Headlice

The first sign that children have headlice is usually when they start scratching their scalp; if you then look closely, you will spot tiny white egg sacs (nits) attached to hair. Headlice are only spread by direct contact.

Treatment Your local pharmacist will advise about headlice treatments currently available, although in many areas these bugs have become immune to standard treatments. For severe cases of headlice, natural pesticides such as quassia, neem oil or tea tree oil can also be used.

5 STEPS TO PREVENT HEADLICE

Community Hygiene Concern recommends this bug-busting routine, which you should carry out regularly whether your child has headlice or not.

1. After **washing hair**, apply conditioner and comb out tangles.
2. Leaving conditioner in hair, to make it slippery, **comb thoroughly** with a nit comb (available from chemists), section by section, working from root to tip. Rinse comb thoroughly between strokes.
3. Rinse hair, leaving it dripping wet, then **repeat the combing** and rinsing process.
4. If there is an outbreak of headlice in your child's class, repeat this routine twice a week for two weeks, then continue to **do it once a week** to help keep nits at bay.
5. Do not forget to **check all other family members** at the same time.

Mosquitoes, gnats and midges

In Britain, the damage mosquitoes cause is limited to an unpleasant bite. They cause most trouble at night, so you should wear insect repellent and cover arms and ankles outside after dark. Mosquitoes hibernate in dark, still sites such as sheds and hollow trees, and breed in stagnant water. Cover water butts and keep drains and gutters clear so they empty quickly. Make sure you renew water in birdbaths regularly.

Treatment Indoors, fit screens to windows if necessary, or use impregnated mosquito coils. This should cope with most cases of gnats and midges as well as mosquitoes, but if mosquitoes from marshland or rivers are a serious problem, contact your environmental health officer.

Traditional remedies Repel mosquitoes by adding a few drops of citronella oil to a saucer of water.

Moths

CLOTHES MOTHS
Adult moths do not damage clothes, but their larvae will eat any natural fibres, and will leave holes in cotton, wool and fur clothing, and in blankets and carpets. The larvae look like small white caterpillars with golden-brown heads.

Treatment Kill larvae by washing everything at the highest recommended temperature, or put in a plastic bag in the freezer for at least 24 hours. Store clean woollen items in sealed polythene bags and spray cupboards with an aerosol suitable for moths. Hang moth repellents in wardrobes, and put sachets such as Colibri Natural Anti-Moth Sachet in drawers. Clean carpets regularly, particularly under heavy furniture, and where carpets meet skirting boards.

FLOUR MOTHS
Flour and other 'stored product' moths generally arrive in the kitchen among poorly stored and transported food. The larvae feed on dry food such as flour, cereals, spices, rice,

▶

lentils, chocolate and nuts, spinning matted webbing as they go. It can be hard to spot their tiny white bodies and brown heads in food, but you may see grey and brown adult moths in the cupboard.

Treatment Throw out affected food and any other open packets of dried food. Empty cupboard and wash and dry it thoroughly before refilling. If you can trace the culprit food, complain to the shop you bought it from.

Rodents

Mice and rats may appear at any time of year. Rodents urinate everywhere they go, spreading disease and food poisoning bacteria, while gnawed cable insulation is a potential fire risk.

MICE
Usually around 4-8cm (1½-3in) long, excluding their tails. Telltale signs of mice include small dark droppings, shredded packaging, nests of paper and a sour smell.

Treatment Contact the pest control division of your local authority's environmental health department or your local pest control company, or you could try using a break-back trap. If mice are a significant problem, however, you must inform your local authority.

RATS
Carry particularly serious illnesses such as the potentially life-threatening Weil's disease. You will probably hear rats scuttling about even if you do not see them as they are large – usually about 23cm (9in) long, excluding the tail, and

weighing around 250g (9oz). Telltale signs of rats include large dark droppings and obvious pilfering of food.

Treatment Contact the pest control division of your local authority's environmental health department or your local pest control company immediately. Do not consider using traps yourself – they will not work.

Silverfish

Silver-coloured and wingless, these fast-moving insects are about 12mm (½in) long and appear in damp areas. They are harmless, although they can damage wallpaper because they feed on starchy substances.

Treatment Correct persistent dampness. If necessary, treat area with an insecticide powder designed to control silverfish or crawling insects.

Wasps

SEE ALSO
Bee and wasp stings,
p.257

Wasps are a nuisance between June and October. Unlike bees, which sting only when provoked and die afterwards, they can sting over and over again, with less provocation. Wasp stings are painful and some people are highly allergic to them. If wasps are all flying to the same spot, look out for the nest – inside a hollow branch, a wall, a shed, in the roof or under the eaves. One nest can produce 30,000 wasps.

Treatment If you discover a nest, contact the pest control division of your local authority's environmental health department or a pest control company. If you only have a small number of wasps, fill a jar with half jam and half water ▶

– wasps love sweet things – and cover with a paper lid punctured with holes. This will attract, trap and drown them. Keep windows closed where possible, or fit fly screens.

Weevils

A type of beetle with a long, pointed snout, around 3.5mm long, they arrive in your home in packets of food and go on to destroy other food stored in the same cupboard. They will be visible in foods such as wholegrain cereals and pasta. Apart from eating your food, weevils – which appear between June and October – are harmless.

Treatment As with flour moths, throw away affected food and other opened packets in the same cupboard – put them in a black bag and take it immediately to your outside dustbin. Empty cupboard and wash and dry it thoroughly before refilling it. If you can trace the culprit food, complain to the shop you bought it from.

Wildlife

You may consider foxes, squirrels or pigeons a nuisance, but it could be illegal to kill them. Contact the pest control division of your local authority's environmental health department or a pest control company, or consult the Department for Environment, Food and Rural Affairs (DEFRA).

Woodlice

Easily recognisable by their grey, segmented bodies, woodlice are 10-15mm (½-¾in) long and have 14 legs. Some types roll into a ball when disturbed. Also known as slaters, sow boys and pill bugs, woodlice live on rotten wood and vegetable matter, occasionally venturing away from their homes under rocks, logs or doormats. They appear between September and April, and do no harm – although they indicate damp.

Treatment In centrally heated houses, the heating will kill them as they cannot live in dry conditions. If you find woodlice a nuisance, treat any damp in the house and use an insecticide powder or long-lasting spray suitable for woodlice, such as Rentokil Insectrol, at their entry point into your house; also, check there is no plant or leaf litter against a wall, making it damp. Fill in any gaps between paving stones.

Woodworm

Woodworm is infestation by any of five different insects – the common furniture beetle, which is the most common and feeds on wood; the death-watch beetle, which infests large old hardwood timbers; the house longhorn beetle, restricted to parts of south-east England; the lyctus powderpost beetle, found in furniture and in block or strip flooring; and the wood-boring weevil, generally found in wet, decaying wood. You can tell if your home is affected by active woodworm by looking for the powdery trains they leave, generally in spring and summer, and holes in furniture. To prevent woodworm, check all second-hand furniture buys for signs of infestation before bringing them into the house.

Treatment Woodworm in furniture can be treated with a proprietary solution or aerosol, available from hardware shops, but specialist treatment is needed if the structural timbers in your home have been affected. Contact the British Wood Preserving and Damp Proofing Association for registered firms.

If things go wrong

IN THIS CHAPTER YOU WILL FIND

In this chapter we give invaluable advice on what to do when things go wrong – including how to find a reputable tradesman in an emergency and how to complain effectively about faulty goods or bad workmanship. You'll also find tips on making a home insurance claim, reading the small print and reporting unfair practices – and a sample letter of complaint.

Complaining

GOLDEN RULES

SEE ALSO
5 Things to do if you are unhappy with a service, p.254

- Make your complaint politely but firmly – in person, by phone or in a brief letter, making it clear what you want and giving a daytime phone number.
- If this doesn't work, make it clear that you are not satisfied and ask to be put in touch with someone senior enough to deal with your complaint (even the MD).
- Tell this person that you expect a response within 14 days – and chase it up if you don't hear from them.
- Keep notes of all visits and phone calls (including names and locations of people you talk to), and copies of letters.
- Be persistent: tell the firm that your problem is theirs, too, until it is sorted out.
- Check whether the firm belongs to an ombudsman or other complaint resolution scheme, and ask them for help. If not, contact your local council's Trading Standards department or a Citizens Advice Bureau.

▶

Address

Date

Dear **(add the name of the managing director, the chief executive or the chairman of the company)**

Knowing that you take a pride in your company's performance, I thought you would like to know that I am currently experiencing/have recently experienced a problem with your product/service from the **(fill in name)** *branch of your company/organisation.*

In essence, the problem is as follows. **(Keep your explanation to a brief outline.)**

The problem began on **(specific date)***. I have made* **(x number)** *attempts to resolve the problem by speaking/telephoning/writing to* **(name)** *at your* **(location)** *branch/office.*

I would appreciate it if you would take the time to investigate this matter and let me know what you plan to do about it.

Yours sincerely

A Reader

cc Good Housekeeping Institute

SAMPLE LETTER OF COMPLAINT (OPPOSITE)

The sample letter opposite shows an approach to adopt when making a complaint. It is important to have a log of the events in order to back up your complaint. Check you have the right contact details for the company.

TAKING YOUR COMPLAINT FURTHER

■ First, let the retailer know as soon as possible that you are unhappy, and give him the chance to put things right.

■ Write a letter setting out your complaint and how you would like to resolve it. Include the following details: what the goods or services are, date purchased, amount paid and payment method. Keep copies.

■ Find out if the trader belongs to a trade association – some offer a free conciliation or arbitration service.

■ You can make a small claim in the County Court (Sheriff Court in Scotland) – you do not need a solicitor. Simply fill in the claim form and send it to the court. There is a fee for this service.

■ If you bought the goods from a website, taking a supplier to court can be difficult. Your contract with the supplier may be subject to the laws of the country from which the item was supplied, rather than subject to British law. The Trading Standards department at your local council will be able to help you in this case.

Emergency repairs

When your central heating packs up or you need a glazier in a hurry, don't panic. Doing a little homework first will save time, money and irritation in the long run.

▶

BEFORE YOU PICK UP THE TELEPHONE

- There is no law against tradesmen increasing their rates in an emergency – if it is 3am and you need someone round immediately, you must expect to pay more. Ask yourself: is this a real emergency or can I find a temporary solution? For example, if the problem is leaking plumbing, turn off the water (make sure you know where the indoor and outdoor stopcocks are).

SEE ALSO

Gas Leaks, p.276
Flooding, p.276

- Do not turn straight to Yellow Pages to find a tradesman – check whether you already have access to any approved tradesmen registers. Ring neighbours or friends for recommendations if you have time. Alternatively, use one of the phone and internet-based services to help you find a tradesman.

- Check that any advertisement you plan to follow up gives the company name, a proper address and fixed phone line.

SEE ALSO

Trade Associations,
p.23

- Do not rely on trade association logos – if you do not have time to check with the relevant association that the company's membership is still valid and what it can do for you if things go wrong, there is no value in using membership as a deciding factor.

TRY THESE OPTIONS FIRST

Home insurance Check your policy – some offer free 24-hour helplines with details of reputable local companies available for emergencies. Even if your policy does not cover the problem, it is worth asking for recommended firms – your insurer will also tell you whether you are covered for damage. It there is a claim it is in the insurer's interest to get the problem fixed quickly and efficiently to save on any related claim for damage.

Maintenance contracts If you have an annual maintenance contract (for your boiler or central heating system, for instance) check if it includes access to the company's approved engineers.

Phone and internet-based services Several websites operate a find-a-tradesman service, a few of which will help put you in touch with those providing an emergency service (see Websites worth a visit, p.22). If you have a problem with electrical or electronic equipment, contact Flying Toolbox – its helpline provides access to around 400 tradesmen vetted and approved by insurers Domestic & General and can tell you which operate over weekends
and/or offer an emergency service.

Utilities companies British Gas and power now offer maintenance contracts on a whole range of household services– domestic appliances, central heating, boilers and controls, house electrics, plumbing and drains.

CHECK WHAT YOU WILL PAY

- Ask what the call-out charge and hourly rate are, and if there is a minimum charge.
- Ask whether you will have to pay the callout charge even if they cannot fix the problem.
- Check the firm is VAT registered – it is a good indicator that it will be reputable. A dead giveaway is the tradesman who offers to work for cash, no questions asked.
- Ask if there is anything you can do before the workman arrives. Never say 'Please, just come now.' And do not be panicked by a trader who suggests that the work should be done urgently when you feel otherwise – always seek a second opinion.

- Do ask for a firm quotation for how much the work will cost, once the tradesman has assessed the job properly. If you decide not to accept the quote, you must pay for whatever initial work has been done (the callout charge plus turning off the stopcock, for instance). It may be that the crisis is averted or you decide you can put up with the inconvenience in the short term and get the rest of the work done more cheaply later.
- Do check carefully everything you are asked to sign. Make sure you get a receipt for all work done and any money you have handed over.

Goods

RETURNING FAULTY GOODS

- If you return faulty goods within a 'reasonable time', you're entitled to a full refund. This period depends on the goods – the time allowed for shoes would be less than that for a major appliance as you would be expected to wear out shoes more quickly. If you are outside the period, you may still be entitled to compensation – usually a repair.
- Your rights are against the retailer you bought from – and that is where you should make your complaint. You may have additional rights against the manufacturer under the guarantee. The guarantee may prove useful if it is too late to reject the goods.
- 'No refunds on sale goods' signs are illegal in the UK. Your rights are the same as at any other time. If you are made aware of the fault when you buy, you can't return it because of that fault.
- You do not need a receipt to return faulty goods – anything that proves you bought it from the shop will do, such as a credit or debit card receipt or statement.

■ Many shops will give you a refund, exchange or credit note if you've changed your mind about something you have bought even if it is not faulty. They are not obliged to do so and may set conditions such as a time limit for returning the goods in question.

Home insurance

MAKING A CLAIM

■ Check the policy covers the cause of damage or loss.

■ Ask your insurer or broker for a claim form, quoting your policy number. Quote the number on all letters, and keep copies of all correspondance.

■ If temporary repairs are needed, arrange these immediately and let your insurer know. Keep all bills and any damaged items as the insurers will probably want to see them. Take photos if necessary. Some insurers offer a 24-hour helpline which can give details of local tradespeople.

■ While waiting for your claim form to arrive, get repair estimates from at least two specialist contractors, list all items lost or damaged, and find original receipts if you can; if not, you should estimate their current value and check the price of replacements.

■ Complete the claim form and return it quickly, with any estimates, receipts and valuations you can to support your case. The insurers will either pay your claim, arrange for their claims inspector to call, or send a loss adjuster to assess the loss or damage. If you need help when making a claim, contact the Association of British Insurers (ABI).

| Rogue traders | Report unfair practices such as misleading mailshots and high-pressure sales tactics to your local council Trading Standards officer, who can use a Stop Now Order. A trader who does not obey the order can be fined or sent to prison. |

| Services | |

Substandard work If the tradesman refuses to put the faults right, do not pay. Say you will get in another firm to assess the value of the work and pay that.

Overcharging If the bill is higher than the amount quoted then refuse to pay the extra unless you changed the specification. If you had a rough estimate you cannot refuse to pay because you think the bill is too high, but tradesmen must set a reasonable price.

5 THINGS TO DO IF YOU ARE UNHAPPY WITH A SERVICE

1. Complain to the **managing director** of the company in writing as well as by phone. Send letters by recorded delivery and keep a copy of all correspondence. Make a note of all phone calls.
2. Contact the **Trading Standards** or Consumer Protection Department at your local council.
3. Check the trade association **code of practice** to see if it offers a conciliation service.
4. If conciliation fails, the association may offer an **arbitration** procedure. You will usually have to pay a token sum towards this, which you forfeit if your claim is rejected. If you accept this arrangement, you may have to agree that the decision is binding and may not be able to take your complaint to court.
5. Consider taking your complaints to the **Small Claims Court** if the total value is less than £1,000. Your local county court will have details of how to proceed.

Small print

Whenever you agree to buy something or order a service, you are making a contract – whether it is written down or not – with whoever is supplying it. Retailers and service providers often use a standard printed contract setting out what they promise to do and what rules you must follow. Read the contract before signing, but even then all the implications may not be obvious. The law says the terms of these contracts must not be unfair – for instance they must not penalise you by a disproportionately large amount if you decide to back out of the deal or try to do away with your right to take them to court in case of any dispute. If you are caught by what seems an unfair term, contact the Office of Fair Trading.

First aid

IN THIS CHAPTER YOU WILL FIND

Here we give step-by-step instructions on how to apply first aid in an emergency, symptoms to look out for, and when to call for an ambulance.

Animal and human bites

1. Wash wound thoroughly with soapy water.
2. Rinse.
3. Dab dry and apply a clean, dry dressing.
4. If wound is deep and or large, go to the Accident and Emergency department of your local hospital as soon as possible, and check tetanus cover (ie when you were last immunised).
5. Report dog bites to the police – rabies is a very serious and potentially fatal infection.

Asthma attack

Call 999 if:

- Patient is having a severe asthma attack that is worse than usual.
- Attack is not relieved by their usual medication.
- It is their first attack.

Bee and wasp stings

1. If sting is still in skin, brush or scrape it off with a fingernail or a blunt knife. Do not use tweezers.
2. Do not squeeze skin; this will spread the venom.
3. Apply a cold compress or ice pack to relieve pain and

▶

reduce swelling – or even a bag of frozen peas covered in a towel.

Call 999 if:

■ Patient suffers a severe allergic reaction.

SYMPTOMS OF SEVERE ALLERGIC REACTION MAY INCLUDE
■ Swollen tongue or lips
■ Wheezing or shortness of breath
■ Rapidly spreading red rash

Bleeding

1. If possible, raise wounded part.
2. Apply pressure to bleeding point with a pad of clean cloth.
3. Apply dressing and bandage firmly. If blood seeps through, put another bandage over the top (do not remove first bandage). If blood comes through both bandages, remove both and reapply new bandage, ensuring it exerts pressure on the bleeding area.
4. Seek medical help.

Broken bones

Take casualty to the Accident and Emergency department of your local hospital.

SIGNS OF A BROKEN BONE INCLUDE
■ Distortion, swelling and bruising at site of injury
■ Pain and difficulty moving injured part

Bee and wasp stings

Burns and scalds

1. Cool area of burn or scald by holding it under a slow-running cold tap, immersing in water or pouring cold water over affected area. Keep burnt area under water for at least 10 minutes, or until pain subsides.
2. Gently remove rings, watches and belts from the casualty before swelling occurs.
3. After cooling, gently remove any clothing that is not sticking to the burnt area.
4. If burn has been caused by chemicals, flood area with water for at least 20 minutes and, wearing protective gloves if available, gently remove contaminated clothing.
5. If burn is not serious, apply a sterile dressing and secure with a bandage – do not use sticking plaster or ointment, or touch the burn with cotton wool or fluffy material.

Send casualty to the Accident and Emergency department of your local hospital, usually by calling 999, if:

- Burn is bigger than the size of the victim's hand.
- Burn is on face, arms, feet or genitals.
- Burn is on a child.

Choking

ADULTS

1. Encourage casualty to try and cough in order to remove the obstruction.
2. Bend casualty forward, and strike up to five times between the shoulder-blades with the heel of your hand. Check mouth for obstruction.
3. If this does not work, stand behind casualty, put one fist between his navel and breast-bone and grasp the fist with your other hand. Pull sharply inwards and upwards up to ▶

five times (this technique is called an abdominal thrust). Recheck mouth.

4. If this does not work, repeat sequence three times, alternating five back slaps with five abdominal thrusts. You must always send casualty to hospital to get checked out if you have done an abdominal thrust.

If casualty loses consciousness, dial 999. Resuscitation may be required.

Repeat steps 1–3 until help arrives.

CHILDREN (1–7 YEARS)

1. Encourage child to cough.
2. Bend child forwards and give up to five slaps between the shoulder blades. Check mouth.
3. If this does not work, stand or kneel behind child and give abdominal thrusts as for adult, but using less pressure.

Dial 999 if this does not work.

Repeat steps 1–2 until help arrives.

INFANTS (0–1 YEAR)

1. Check mouth.
2. Lay infant face down along your forearm and slap firmly between the shoulder-blades. Repeat up to five times. Check mouth and remove obstruction with one finger.
3. If this does not work, lay the infant on its back on your arm or lap.
4. Using two fingers, press down in middle of chest, one finger's width below nipple. Press sharply up to five times (this is called a chest thrust). You must always send casualty to hospital to get checked out if you have done a chest thrust.
5. Check again for obstruction, and remove if possible. Check mouth again.

Dial 999 if this does not work.
Repeat steps 1–4 until help arrives.

Cuts and grazes

1. Rinse with running water to clean dirt and grit.
2. Dab dry and apply sterile dressing. Do not use creams or ointments.
3. Check tetanus cover (ie when patient was last immunised).
4. Get person to consult their GP if cut oozes pus or is sore and inflamed.

Send casualty to the Accident and Emergency department of your local hospital if:

■ Cut is deep.

Electric shock

1. Look at the casualty first, don't touch.
2. Check the power is off.
3. Once you are sure the casualty is away from the source of electricity, check their breathing and circulation.
4. Rescusitation may be required.

Send casualty to the Accident and Emergency department of your local hospital.

Fainting

1. Get casualty to lie down flat if not already on the ground.
2. Kneel down in front of them and support their raised legs by putting their ankles on your shoulder.
3. Make sure there is plenty of fresh air in room – open windows if necessary.

Fits

Do not restrain patient, but try to prevent any injuries.

Call 999 if:

■ The patient is fitting and is not known to be epileptic.

■ The patient is an epileptic and the fit is lasting longer than usual.

Minor wounds

1. Raise and support injured part if possible, and apply direct pressure to wound.
2. Protect wound with an adhesive plaster or sterile dressing.
3. Check tetanus cover (ie when patient was last immunised).

Send casualty to the Accident and Emergency department of your local hospital if:

■ Any object is embedded in wound. Do not remove it yourself.

■ Bleeding does not stop.

Nosebleeds

1. Get person to sit down and lean forward.
2. Ask them to breathe through their mouth and squeeze the soft part of their nose for at least 10 minutes.
3. Reassure and help them if necessary.

Send casualty to the Accident and Emergency department of your local hospital if:

■ Nosebleed is severe or lasts more than 30 minutes.

Poisoning or overdose

Send casualty to the Accident and Emergency department of your local hospital but first:

Fainting

- Try to discover what they have swallowed.
- Send remains of poison with them, eg the bottle, etc.
- Resuscitation may be required if casualty collapses.

Rash

Send casualty to the Accident and Emergency department of your local hospital immediately if rash does not fade under pressure.

- Inform the Accident and Emergency department of your local hospital department of possible diagnosis of meningitis.

SIGNS AND SYMPTOMS OF MENINGITIS MAY INCLUDE ANY OF THE FOLLOWING:
- High temperature
- Vomiting
- Severe headache
- Neck stiffness
- Joint or muscle pains
- Drowsiness
- Confusion
- Dislike of bright lights
- Seizures
- Rash

Shock

1. Loosen the casualty's clothing and lay them down, raising their legs if possible.
2. Keep the casualty warm by wrapping a blanket or coat around them; however do not use hot water bottles or a heater to warm them.
3. Moisten lips with water, but do not give casualty a drink or anything to eat or smoke.
4. Check and record the casualty's breathing and pulse frequently.
5. Reassure casualty and make them comfortable.
6. Seek medical attention if necessary by calling 999.

▶

Splinters

1. Clean area with soap and water.
2. Sterilise pair of tweezers by passing them through flame from a match or lighter, and allow to cool.
3. Do not touch ends of tweezers, or wipe away soot.
4. Holding tweezers as close as possible to skin, but without touching, grip end of splinter and gently pull out,
5. Carefully squeeze wound to encourage a little bleeding.
6. Clean and dry area and apply adhesive dressing.
7. If splinter breaks, go to the Accident and Emergency department of your local hospital or your GP.

Sunburn and windburn

1. Cover skin with light clothing or a towel.
2. Remove casualty to shade.
3. Cool affected area by sponging with cold water, and give sips of water.
4. Do not break blisters.
5. For mild burns, put on calamine lotion or an after-sun preparation.
6. If burns are severe, get medical aid.

FIRST AID COURSES AND KITS
St John Ambulance holds First Aid courses throughout the country – call 08700 10 49 50 or visit the website at www.sja.org.uk for details. To order a First Aid kit from St John Supplies, call 020 7278 7888 or e-mail customer.services@stjohnsupplies.co.uk for details.

Directory

Good Housekeeping has a policy of featuring only goods and services available in high streets throughout the UK or by mail order or the internet. While we have done our best to ensure that firms and organisations mentioned in Home Handbook are reputable, we can give no guarantee that they will fulfil their obligations under all circumstances. Readers must be prepared to deal with the firms and organisations at their own risk.

APPLIANCE MANUFACTURERS

AEG
Tel: 0870 535 0350; www.aeg.co.uk
Baumatic
Tel: 0118 933 6900; www.baumatic.com
Belling
Tel: 0116 212 3456;
www.bellingappliances.co.uk
Beko
Tel: 01923 818121; www.beko.co.uk
Bosch
Tel: 0870 727 0446;
www.boschappliances.co.uk
Brandt
Tel: 01256 308000; www.Brandt.com
Braun
Tel: 0800 783 7010; www.braun.com
Breville
Tel: 0800 525 089; www.breville.co.uk
Bush
Tel: 020 8787 3111
Cannon
Tel: 0870 154 6474; www.cannongas.co.uk

CFM Kinder
Tel: 01782 339000; www.gas-fires.co.uk
Creda
Tel: 0870 154 6474; www.creda.co.uk
De Dietrich
Tel: 0870 750 3503; www.dedietrich.co.uk
DeLonghi
Tel: 0845 600 6845; www.delonghi.co.uk
Domena
Tel: 01825 749498; www.domena.com
Dualit
Tel: 01293 652500; www.dualit.com
Electrolux
Tel: 0870 595 0950; www.electrolux.co.uk
Fisher and Paykel
Tel: 01926 626700; www.fisherpaykel.co.uk
Gaggia
Tel: 01422 330295; www.gaggia.uk.com
Haier
Tel: 01527 578333; www.haiereurope.com
Hitachi
Tel: 01628 643000;
www.hitachi-consumer-eu.com

Hoover-Candy
Tel: 01685 721222; www.hoovercandy.co.uk
Hotpoint
Tel: 0870 150 6070; www.hotpoint.co.uk
JVC
Tel: 0870 330 5000; www.jvc.co.uk
Kenwood
Tel: 02392 392333; www.kenwood.co.uk
Kitchen Aid
Tel: 0845 450 0099
Lec
Tel: 01243 863161; www.lec.co.uk
LG
Tel: 0870 607 5544; www.lge.co.uk
Liebherr
Tel: 01977 665665; www.lhg.liebherr.de
Magimix
Tel: 01483 427411
Maytag
Tel: 01737 231000; www.maytag-uk.com
Miele
Tel: 01235 554455; www.miele.co.uk
Morphy Richards
Tel: 08450 777 700;
www.morphyrichards.co.uk
Neff
Tel: 0870 513 3090; www.neff.co.uk
Panasonic
Tel: 08705 357 357; www.panasonic.co.uk
Philips
Tel: 0845 601 0354; www.philips.co.uk
Polti
Tel: 0800 132509; www.polti-ltd.co.uk
Prima
Tel: 0113 251 1500;
www.prima-international.com
Rangemaster
Tel: 01926 457400; www.rangemaster.co.uk

Rowenta
Tel: 0845 602 1454; www.rowenta.co.uk
Russell Hobbs
Tel: 0161 947 3170; www.saltoneurope.com
Samsung
Tel: 0800 521652;
www.samsungelectronics.co.uk
Sanyo
Tel: 01923 246 363; www.sanyo.co.uk
Scandinova
Tel: 0845 600 7002; www.comet.co.uk
Servis
Tel: 0121 568 8333; www.servisuk.co.uk
Sharp
Tel: 0800 262958; www.sharp.co.uk
Smeg
Tel: 0870 990 9908; www.smeguk.com
Sony
Tel: 08705 111999; www.sony.co.uk
Stoves
Tel: 0151 426 6551; www.stoves.co.uk
Tefal
Tel: 0845 602 1454; www.tefal.co.uk
Vax
Tel: 0870 606 1248; www.vax.co.uk
Whirlpool
Tel; 0870 600 8989; www.whirlpool.co.uk
White Knight
Tel: 01422 203585; www.crosslee.co.uk

PRODUCTS

Most products mentioned in this book are
available at supermarkets, hardware stores,
department stores and specialist outlets.

1001
Tel: 0161 491 8000; www.pzcussons.com
Carpet and upholstery cleaner.

Antiquax
Tel: 0161 6270983; www.jamesbriggs.co.uk
Wax polish for furniture and floors, and crystal and chandelier cleaner.
Astonish
Tel: 0113 236 0036;
www.astonishcleaners.com
Cleaning product for household surfaces.
Bar Keepers Friend
Tel: 0208 8715027;
www.homecareproducts.co.uk
Stain remover for household surfaces.
Bell
Tel: 01604 777500; www.abell.co.uk
Kitchen and bathroom appliances.
Bin Fresh
Tel: 0870 6030420; www.challs.com
Cleaner and deodoriser for household bins.
Bissell
Tel: 0870 225 0109
Carpet and upholstery cleaner.
Cat Mate
Tel: 01932 700001; www.pet-mate.com
Automatic pet feeder.
Colibri
Tel: 020 8761 9250
Natural pest repellents.
ColorFill
Tel: 0191 259 0033; www.unika.co.uk
Sealant for floors and work surfaces.
Con-ex
Tel: 01636 613609; www.allerayde.co.uk
Allergy control home products.
Copes
Tel: 020 8803 6481; www.copes.co.uk
Supplier of soft furnishings and blind cleaners.

Crucial Trading
Tel: 01562 743747; www.crucial-trading.com
Natural flooring suppliers.
Cuprinol
Tel: 01753 550555; www.cuprinol.co.uk
Wood preservatives and mould inhibitors.
Dasco
Tel: 01536 760760; www.dunkelman.com
Fabric cleaner for leather and suede.
Deofab
Tel: 020 8332 1515; www.msg.co.uk
Fabric deodoriser.
De.Solv.It
Tel: 01933 402822; www.mykal.co.uk
Natural citrus stain remover.
Dettox
Tel: 0500 646645; www.reckittbenckiser.com
Disinfectant.
Dylon
Tel: 020 8663 4296; www.dylon.co.uk
For colour-run remover, net curtain whitener and fabric stain remover.
Febreze
Tel: 0800 3282882; www.pg.com
Eliminates odour on most types of fabric.
Fila
Tel: 01438 317712; www.agceramics.co.uk
E-mail: info@agceramics.co.uk
For household tiling products.
FreshenUp
Tel: 0800 7316165; www.backtonature.com
Deodorising spray.
Goddards
Tel: 01276 852000; www.scjohnson.com/uk
Silver polish.

Grangers
Tel: 01773 521521; www.stay-dry.co.uk
E-mail: info@grangers.co.uk
Cleaning and waterproofing sprays for smooth leather, nubuck, suede and fabric Gore-Tex footwear.

Hammerite
Tel: 01661 830 000; www.hammerite.com
Products for cleaning metal surfaces.

Hamster Baskets
Tel: 01531 670209;
www.hamsterbaskets.co.uk
Pet baskets and cages.

Help!
Tel: 01444 244000; www.bio-productions.co.uk
Pet stain remover for carpets.

HG Hageson
Tel: 01206 795200;
www.HGinternational.com
E-mail: info@hgesan.co.uk
Suppliers of tiling products and plastic furniture cleaner.

Hob Brite
Tel: 020 8871 5027;
www.homecareproducts.co.uk
Cleaner for ceramic and halogen hobs.

International Paint Ltd
Tel: 01480 484284;
www.international-paints.co.uk
Primers and paints.

K2r
Tel: 01905 450300; www.spontex.co.uk
E-mail: webmail@spontex.co.uk
Stain remover spray for dry-clean-only fabrics, upholstery and carpets.

Kiwi/Kiwi Select
Tel: 01536 760760; www.dunkelman.com
Fabric and shoe cleaner for leather and suede.

Leather Master
Tel: 0115 946 0274; www.leathermasteruk.com
E-mail: info@LeatherMasterUK.com
Cleaning products for leather, suede and nubuck

Liberon
Tel: 01797 367 555
For wax and restoration products.

Lithofin
Tel: 0800 085 4547; www.expensive.co.uk
Cleaning products for marble.

Loctite
Tel: 01707 358844; www.loctite.co.uk
Adhesives and adhesive removers.

Lord Sheraton
Tel: 020 8663 4296; www.dylon.co.uk
Wood and leather care.

Mauviel Cuprinox
Tel: 01922 416555; www.cookcraft.com
Copper cleaner for kitchenware.

Milton
Tel: 01202 780558
Sterilising fluid.

Minky
Tel: 01706 353535; www.minky.com
For cleaning, laundry care and textile products.

Mr Muscle
Tel: 01276 852000; www.scjohnson.com
Multi purpose kitchen cleaners.

Mystox
Tel: 020 8202 8972
Fungicide.

Neutradol
Tel: 020 83321515; www.msg.co.uk
Deodorisers.

Nikwax
Tel: 01550 740655; www.calamander.co.uk
Cleaning, waterproofing and protection for clothing, footwear, tents and equipment.

Nilco
Tel: 01256 474661; www.solvitol.com
Cleaning spray for UPVC.

Nippon
Tel: 01530 510060; www.vitax.co.uk
Ant repellents.

Olbas Oil
Tel: 01452 524012; www.laneshealth.com
Eucalyptus oil.

Oust
Tel: 020 8663 4296; www.dylon.co.uk
Descalers.

Plasti-Kote
Tel: 01223 836400; www.spraypaint.co.uk
E-mail: sales@plasti-kote.co.uk
Decorative and DIY spray paints.

Raid
Tel: 01276 852000; www.scjohnson.com/uk
Insect repellents.

Rustins
Tel: 020 8450 4666; www.rustins.co.uk
For decorating, paint and varnish products.

Scotchgard
Tel: 08705 360036; www.3m.com
Rug and carpet cleaner.

Shaws
Tel: 01296 429333; www.shawspet.co.uk
Pet stain remover for carpets.

Silvo
Tel: 0845 769 7079;
www.reckittbenckiser.com
Silver cleaner (jewellery and household items).

Sparkle
Tel: 01276 852000; www.scjohnson.com/uk
Furniture polishes.

Spot Shot
Tel: 01204 600500; www.acdoco.co.uk
Carpet stain remover.

Stain Devils
Tel: 01204 600500; www.acdoco.co.uk
Fabric and stain remover.

Stain Slayer
Tel: 01243 531319
Fabric and stain remover.

Swarfega
Tel: 01773 596700; www.deb.co.uk
Hand cleaning gel.

Town Talk
Tel: 01204 520014; www.towntalkpolish.com
Metal polish and jewellery cleaner.

Vanish
Tel: 0845 769 7079; www.reckittbenckiser.com
Stain remover for carpets, upholstery and
fabrics.

Wenko
Tel: 01438 759 880; www.wenko.de
Iron soleplate cleaner.

White Wizard
Tel: 015394 88100; www.lakelandlimited.co.uk
Fabric stain remover.

Wine Away
Tel: 015394 88100; www.wineawayuk.co.uk
Red wine stain remover, available from
Lakeland Limited.

Woolite
Tel: 0845 769 7079; www.reckittbenckiser.com
Stain remover for woollen fabrics and carpets.

X=O
Tel: 01903 733377; www.geniecare.com
Odour neutraliser.

Zebo
Tel: 0845 769 7079; www.reckittbenckiser.com
Household polish for metal surfaces

▶

MANUFACTURERS, SUPPLIERS, SERVICE PROVIDERS AND RETAILERS

Acton and Acton Ltd
Tel: 01706 656972;
www.actonandactonltd.co.uk
For special-sized bedding.

Antique Brass Bedstead Company
Tel: 01245 471137;
www.LLph.co.uk/bedsteads.htm
For antique brass beds.

The Bathing Machine
Tel: 01132 702534;
www.thebathingmachine.com
For bathroom fittings in different colours.

Bathroom Renovations Ltd
Tel: 020 8894 6464;
www.bathrenovationltd.co.uk
Offers a re-enamelling service.

Bed Bazaar
Tel: 01728 723756
For antique brass beds.

Bernards
Tel: 0151 6523136; www.bernards.co.uk
Supplier of PVD door furniture.

Betterware
Tel: 0500 555667; www.betterware.co.uk
Supplier of Sticky Stuff stain removal.

British Gas
Tel: 0845 600 5100; www.house.co.uk
Energy provider and service contracts.

Chinamatch
Tel: 01905 391520; www.chinamatch.uk.com
E-mail: chinamatchuk@compuserve.com
For matching china.

China Matching Service
Tel: 01548 531372
www.chinamatchingservice.co.uk
E-mail: enquiries@chinamatchingservice.co.uk
For matching china.

China Set and Match
Tel: 01306 730757
For matching china.

Chortex
Tel: 01204 695611; www.chortex.com
Supplier of extra large bath sheets.

Comet
Tel: 0845 600 7002; www.comet.co.uk
Retailer of household electrical appliances.

Conservation by Design
Tel: 01234 853555
www.conservation-by-design.co.uk
For acid-reduced cardboard and acid-free tissue

Dixons/Currys
Tel: 0845 8500535; www.currys.co.uk
Retailer of household electrical appliances.

Domestic & General
Tel: 0870 607 5566; www.domgen.com
For a multi-appliance insurance policy.

Dyno-Rod
Tel: 0800 316 4599; www.dyno.com
Specialist drain services.

The Eiderdown Studio
Tel: 01395 271147
Offers a service to recover worn duvets.

Facets
Tel: 020 85203392; www.facetsglass.co.uk
For glass restoration.

Forneaux de France
Tel: 01202 733011; www.fdef.co.uk
Supplier of traditional ranges with separate grill

Georgina's Shoes
Tel: 020 8882 7215; www.katekuba.com
Offers a shoe dye service.
Giltbrook Cleaners and Dyers
Tel: 01159 382 231;
www.giltbrookcleaners.co.uk
Offers a clothes dye service.
Givans
Tel: 020 7352 6352
Offers a service to recover worn duvets.
Harry Berger
Tel: 0161 485 3421/7733
Offers a clothes dye service.
Helen Warren China Restoration
Tel: 01580 895100;
www.ifwarren.demon.co.uk
E-mail: conservation@ifwarren.demon.co.uk
For china restoration.
Horrocks Shades
Tel: 01492 533105;
www.horrocksshades.co.uk
Lampshade re-covering service.
Inter-Bath Restoration Services
Tel: 0800 026 0070
Bath re-enamelling service.
Ivory
Tel: 020 7408 1266; www.ivoryshoes.com
Shoe dye service.
J. Barbour
Tel: 01914554444; www.barbour.com
Rewaxing, repairing and reproofing Barbour
jackets.
Jeeves of Belgravia
Tel: 020 8809 3232;
www.jeevesofbelgravia.co.uk
Vacuum packing service.

Johnson Apparel Master
Tel: 0191 482 0088
Offers a service to recover worn duvets.
Jonelle/John Lewis
Tel: 0845 6049049; www.johnlewis.com
John Lewis brand name; products include
cleaner for polished stainless steel cookware.
Keys of Clacton
Tel: 01255 432518; www.keysbedding.co.uk
For special-size bedding.
Lakeland Ltd
Tel: 015394 88100; www.lakelandlimited.com
For Magic Balls glass cleaners.
Leather Master
Tel: 0115 946 0274;
www.leathermasteruk.com
E-mail: info@LeatherMasterUK.com
M. Brock Ltd
Tel: 01508 531999; www.mbrock.co.uk
Supplier of PVD door furniture.
Mappin and Webb
Tel: 020 7734 3801;
www.mappin-and-webb.co.uk
For glass engraving.
Nisbets
Tel: 01454 855555; www.nisbets.com
Heat diffusers for hobs.
Norwich Union Direct
Tel: 0800 888777
For multi-appliance insurance.
Oxford China Restoration Studio
Tel: 01865 376 046
www.oxfordchinarestorationstudio.co.uk
For china restoration.
Phil Green and Son
Tel: 01885 488936;
www.philgreenandson.co.uk
Suppliers of reconditioned agas.

Redhouse Glass Crafts
Tel: 01384 399460
www.antiques.ukdealers.com/redhouse
For glass restoration.
Rentokil
Tel: 01342 833022; www.rentokil-initial.com
Pest control.
Renubath Services Ltd
Tel: 01285 656624/020 7381 8337
www.renubath.co.uk
Bath re-enamelling service.
Safe Storage Company Ltd
Tel: 01614 853421
For acid-reduced cardboard and acid-free
tissue.
Samuel Heath
Tel: 0121 766 4200; www.samuel-heath.com
Supplier of PVD door furniture.
Scotchcare Services
Tel: 0800 581 546; www.scotchcare.co.uk
E-mail: info@scotchcare.co.uk
Network of franchised carpet and upholstery
cleaning and protection firms.
ServiceMaster
Tel: 0116 236 4646; www.servicemaster.co.uk
Network of franchised carpet and upholstery
cleaning firms.
SF Detection
Tel: 0800 0642 999; www.sfdetection.com
E-mail: sales@sfdetection.com
Supplier of carbon monoxide alarms.
Tablewhere?
Tel: 020 8361 6111; www.tablewhere.co.uk
E-mail: info@tablewhere.co.uk
For matching china.
Thomas Goode & Co Ltd
Tel: 020 7499 2823; www.thomasgoode.co.uk
For glass engraving.

Trent Bathrooms
Tel: 01274 521199;
www.shires-bathrooms.com
For bathroom fittings in discontinued colours.
Twyford Cookers
Tel: 01432355924; www.twyford-cookers.com
Suppliers of reconditioned agas.
The White Company
Tel: 0870 1601610; www.thewhiteco.com
For extra large bath sheets.
Wilds Table Felts
Tel: 01204 399593;
www.tablecare.fsbusiness.co.uk
For heat-resistant mats to place under table
cloths.
Wilkinson
Tel: 020 8314 1080; www.wilkinson-plc.com
For glass restoration.

USEFUL ORGANISATIONS
This list includes consumer watchdogs, advice
agencies, trade associations and other non-
commercial organisations.

Advertising Standards Authority (ASA)
Tel: 020 7580 5555; www.asa.org.uk
Allergy UK
Tel: 020 8303 8583 (helpline)
www.allergyuk.org
E-mail: info@allergyuk.org
The Association of British Insurers (ABI)
Tel: 020 7600 3333; www.abi.org.uk
E-mail: info@abi.org.uk
Association of British Pewter Craftsmen
Tel: 0114 252 7550; www.abpcltd.co.uk
E-mail: enquiries@abpcltd.co.uk
Association of Master Upholsterers
Tel: 016 3321 5454; www.upholsterers.co.uk
E-mail: info@upholsterers.co.uk

Bathroom Manufacturers' Association
Tel: 01782 747123; www.bathroom-association.org
British Antique Furniture Restorers' Association
Tel: 01305 854822; www.bafra.org.uk
E-mail: headoffice@bafra.org.uk
British Audio Dealers' Association
Tel: 01737 760008; www.bada.co.uk
British Carpet Manufacturers' Association
Tel: 01562 755568;
www.carpetfoundation.com
E-mail: rupertanton@carpetfoundation.com
British Cutlery and Silverware Association
Tel: 0114 252 7550
British Pest Control Association
Tel: 01332 294288; www.bpca.org.uk
British Red Cross
Tel: 020 7235 5454; www.redcross.org.uk
E-mail: enquiries@redcross.org.uk
British Wood Preserving and Damp Proofing Association
Tel: 01332 225100; www.bwpda.co.uk
E-mail: info@bwpda.co.uk
BT Malicious Calls Advice Line
Tel: 0800 666700
BT Malicious Calls Bureau
Tel: 0800 661441
Central Heating Information Council
Tel: 01926 430 486;
www.centralheating.co.uk
E-mail: info@centralheating.co.uk
Citizens Advice
Telephone your local bureau direct.
www.adviceguide.org.uk
Community Hygiene Concern
Tel: 02076864321; www.chc.org
E-mail: bugbusters2k@yahoo.co.uk

Council for Registered Gas Installers (CORGI)
Tel: 01256 372 200; www.corgi-gas.com
E-mail: enquiries@corgi-gas.com
Department for Environment, Food and Rural Affairs (DEFRA)
Tel: 08459 33 55 77 (helpline);
www.defra.gov.uk
E-mail: helpline@defra.gsi.gov.uk
Disabled Living Foundation
Tel: 0845 130 9177; www.dlf.org.uk
E-mail: info@dlf.org.uk
The Disabled Living Centres Council
Tel: 0161 834 1044; www.dlcc.org.uk
E-mail: dlcc@dlcc.org.uk
Dry Cleaning Information Bureau
Tel: 020 8863 8658; www.tsa-uk.org
Electrical Contractors' Association (ECA)
Tel: 020 7313 4800; www.eca.co.uk
E-mail Preference Service
Energywatch
Tel: 0845 906 0708; www.energywatch.org.uk
E-mail: enquiries@energywatch.org.uk
Fax Preference Service
Tel: 020 7291 3330
Federation of Master Builders
Tel: 020 7242 7583; www.fmb.org.uk
E-mail: central@fmb.org.uk
Floodline
Tel: 0845 988 1188;
www.environmentagency.co.uk
Flying Toolbox
Tel: 0870 600 0961; www.flyingtoolbox.com
E-mail: info@flyingtoolbox.com
Furniture Industry and Research Association (FIRA)
Tel: 01438 777700; www.fira.co.uk
Heating and Ventilating Contractors' Association
Tel: 020 7313 4900; www.hvca.org.uk ▶

Home Laundering Consultative Council
Tel: 020 7636 7788

Homepro
Tel: 0870 734 4344; www.homepro.com

Improveline
www.improveline.com

Independent Committee for the Supervision of Standards of Telephone Information Services (ICSTIS)
Tel: 0800 500212; www.icstis.org.uk

Institute of Paper Conservation
Tel: 01886 832 323; www.ipc.org.uk
E-mail: information@ipc.org.uk

Institute of Plumbing
Tel: 01708 472791; www.plumbers.org.uk
E-mail: info@plumbers.org.uk

Kitchen Specialists Association (KSA)
Tel: 01905 726066 (consumer helpline)
www.kbsa.co.uk
E-mail: info@kbsa.co.uk

Mailing Preference Service
Tel: 020 7291 3310

National Association of Councils for Voluntary Service
Tel: 01142 786636; www.nacvs.org.uk

National Asthma Campaign
Tel: 020 7226 2260; www.asthma.org.uk

National Bed Federation
Tel: 01823 368008; www.bedfed.org.uk

National Carpet Cleaners' Association Ltd (NCCA)
Tel: 0116 271 9550; www.ncca.co.uk
E-mail: officencca.aol.com

National Federation of Roofing Contractors
Tel: 020 7436 0387; www.nfrc.co.uk

NHS Direct (Essential phone numbers)
Tel: 0845 46 47; www.nhsdirect.nhs.uk

National Inspection Council for Electrical Installation Contracting (NICEIC)
Tel: 020 7564 2323; www.niceic.org.uk

National Institute of Carpet and Floor Layers (formerly the National Institute of Carpet Fitters)
Tel: 01159583077; www.nicfltd.org.uk
E-mail: info@nicltd.org.uk

npower
Tel: 01793 877777; www.npower.com
E-mail: helpline@npower.com

Office of Fair Trading
Tel: 0845 7224499 or 0870 606 0321
www.oft.gov.uk
E-mail: enquiries@oft.gsi.gov.uk

Ofgem
Tel: 0207 9017000; www.ofgem.gov.uk
E-mail: mailing@ofgem.gov.uk

Oftel
Tel: 0845 714 5000; www.oftel.gov.uk
E-mail: infocent@oftel.gov.uk

Oxfam
Tel: 0870 010 1049; www.oxfam.org.uk
E-mail: oxfam@oxfam.org.uk

Postwatch
Tel: 08456 013265; www.postwatch.co.uk

Qualitas
Tel: 01438 777770; www.fira.co.uk
E-mail: qualitas@fira.co.uk

Quality Guild
Tel: 0870 757 1188; www.quality-guild.co.uk

Quality Mark
Tel: 0845 300 8040; www.qualitymark.org.uk

Ricability
Tel: 020 7427 2460; www.ricability.org.uk
E-mail: mail@ricability.org.uk

Royal National Institute For the Blind (RNIB)
0845 766 9999; www.rnib.org.uk
E-mail: helpline@rnib.org.uk

Royal School of Needlework
Tel: 020 8943 1432;
www.royal-needlework.co.uk
E-mail: enquiries@royal-needlework.co.uk
Scope
Tel: 020 7619 7100; www.scope.org.uk
E-mail: cphelpline@scope.org.uk
ServiceMaster
Tel: 01792 776 333; www.servicemaster.co.uk
E-mail: webmaster@servicemaster.co.uk
Skills Register
Tel: 01342 305 900; www.skills-register.com
E-mail: enqs@skills-register.com
Solid Fuel Association
Tel: 0800 600000; www.solidfuel.co.uk
E-mail: sfa@solidfuel.co.uk
St John Ambulance
Tel: 08700 10 49 50; www.london.sja.org.uk
Stone Federation of Great Britain
Tel: 020 7608 5094; www.stone-
federationgb.org.uk
Telephone Preference Service
Tel: 020 7291 3320
Trading Standards
www.tradingstandards.gov.uk
www.consumercomplaints.org.uk
Transco (Essential phone numbers)
Tel: 0121 626 4431; www.transco.co.uk
Trust UK
Tel: 020 7291 3345; www.trustuk.org.uk
Victoria & Albert Museum
Tel: 020 7942 2000; www.vam.ac.uk
E-mail: vanda@vam.ac.uk (general enquiries)
Vitreous Enamel Association
Tel: 07071 226716; www.ive.org.uk
WaterVoice
Tel: 0121 625 1300; www.watervoice.org.uk

YOUR.ESSENTIAL PHONE NUMBERS

HOUSEHOLD

GAS LEAKS
If you think you can smell gas, turn off the gas supply at the meter, open all doors and windows and check boiler pilot light is out. **Ring the free Transco emergency helpline on 0800 111 999.** Until the all-clear, do not smoke, use a naked flame or turn the electricity on or off.

FLOODING
Find out what precautions to take, and what to do in the event of flooding, by ringing the Environment Agency's Floodline for England, Scotland and Wales on 0845 988 1188, or Northern Ireland on 02890 253195.

GAS SUPPLIER

ELECTRICITY SUPPLIER

POLICE STATION

GLAZIER

ELECTRICIAN

LOCKSMITH

PLUMBER

CREDIT CARD PROTECTION

INSURANCE COMPANIES

INSURANCE POLICY NUMBERS

SOLICITOR

MEDICAL

EMERGENCIES
If you are registered with a doctor or dentist, you are entitled to emergency treatment, so ring the practice for details of its emergency rota.

MEDICAL HELPLINE
Ring NHS Direct on 0845 46 47   www.nhsdirect.nhs.uk

DOCTOR

DENTIST

HOSPITAL

VET

Family's blood groups

Healthcare insurance company

Healthcare insurance number

Medical card numbers

National insurance numbers

OTHER CONTACT NUMBERS

Index

▶

▶

freestanding cookers 34–5
microwave ovens 96–9, 148
range cookers 35–6
overdoses, first aid 263
overflow pipes, dripping 224–5
Oxfam 230
ozone-depleting gases, disposal of
fridges and freezers 229

P
paint
cleaning paintwork 133
disposal of paint tins 230
drying times 68
estimating quantities 68
stain removal 189–90, 203
painting
problem solver 226
tiles 224
paintings
cleaning 131
hanging 225
pans 93–6
cleaning 148–50
coatings 95
dishwasher-proof 44
features 96
and hobs 94
materials 93–5
paper, in microwave ovens 97
paper adhesives, stain removal 188
parchment lampshades, cleaning
127
paring knives 92
parquet floors 51
pasta machines, cleaning 150
patent leather 160–1
patio heaters 83–5
patios, cleaning 118–19
payments
for emergency repairs 250, 251
kitchen installation 58
overcharging 254
to tradesmen 25
pearls, cleaning 146
peeling wallpaper 227
pens, stain removal 190, 196, 210,
212
percale 163
perfume, stain removal 203
pests 234–45
petrol
disposal of 229
lawnmowers 82
pets
deodorisers 180
hairs on upholstery 184–5
stain removal 189

stray cats 233
vacuum cleaners 107
pewter, cleaning 129
phones see telephones
pictures
cleaning 131
hanging 225
pigeons 244
pillows
care and cleaning 175–6
dustmites 237, 238
pipes
blockages 220
dripping overflow pipes 224–5
planning permission 25
plasma screen televisions 102
plastics
chopping boards 91, 115
handbags 182
lampshades 127
in microwave ovens 97
platform-top bed bases 29
plumbing
blockages 217, 220
emergency repairs 250
trade associations 23
pocketed spring mattresses 30
poisoning, first aid 263
polish
furniture 125
linoleum 120
wooden floors 122–3
pollen stains 203, 211, 213
polyamide
carpets 47
fabrics 163
polyester
bags 182
carpets 47
fabrics 163
pillows 176
polyethylene chopping boards 91
polypropylene
carpets 47
chopping boards 91
suitcases 182
poplin 163
post, junk mail 231
poster paints, stain removal 190
pottery, in microwave ovens 97
powder paints, stain removal 190
power showers 28
price-matching pledges 15
problem solving 214–64
public liability insurance 25
PVC fabrics 164
PVCU doors, cleaning 118
Pyrex, in microwave ovens 97
pyrolytic oven cleaners 42

Q
Qualitas 67
quarry tiles 50
cleaning 122
quilts 173–4
quotations
for emergency repairs 252
and insurance claims 253
kitchen installation 58
and overcharging 254
from tradesmen 22, 24

R
radiant fires, cleaning 142
radiant hobs 38
choosing pans 94
cleaning 117
radiators, bleeding 223–4
radio, stereo systems 101
raffia lampshades, cleaning 127
rainwear 182
range cookers 35–6
choosing pans 94
rashes, first aid 263
rats 242–3
rattan garden furniture 85
Rayburn ranges 36
choosing pans 94
rayon 167
RCDs (residual current devices) 82
RDS (Radio Data System) 101
receipts
faulty goods 252
from tradesmen 25
recirculating cooker hoods 41
recycling facilities 231
red wine stains 204, 211, 213
refrigerators see fridges
refunds
home shopping 12
internet shopping 13
price-matching pledges 15
returning faulty goods 252–3
regulators, patio heaters 84
remote control, stereo systems 101
repairs
emergency 249–52
extended warranties 15–18
resin garden furniture 85
cleaning 125
retailers
complaints 247–9
directory of 270–2
faulty goods 12, 252–3
price-matching pledges 15
small print 255
your rights 11, 12
ring marks, on furniture 222–3
RMS, stereo systems 101

rodents 242–3
rogue traders 254
roller blinds 58, 176–7
Roman blinds 58
roofing contractors, trade
    associations 23
rotary lawnmowers 81
rotisseries 37
Royal National Institute for the
    Blind 230
rubber floors 50
rubbish disposal 228–31
rubies, cleaning 146
rugs, sheepskin 164
runs, in paintwork 226
rush matting 50
    cleaning 121
rust stains 204–5, 213

S
Sabatier knives 92
safety
    carbon monoxide 34
    food preparation 78
    patio heaters 83
    smoke alarms 104
St John Ambulance 261
sales, faulty goods 12, 252
salt marks, removal 205
sapphires, cleaning 146
satin 164
saucepans see pans
sauces, stain removal 199–200
Saxony carpets 46
scalds, first aid 259
SCART plugs
    DVD players 100
    televisions 103–4
Scope 230
scorch marks, removal 205–6
scratches
    on acrylic baths 111
    on electrical appliances 220
    on furniture 222–3
screens, television 102–3, 104
seagrass floor covering 50
    cleaning 106, 121
sealants
    cleaning 112
    cracked 217
sealed hotplates 38
    choosing pans 94
    cleaning 117
second-hand beds 31
security, internet shopping 13
self-undercoat gloss paint 68
serrated knives 92
services
    complaints 254

directory 270–2
    overcharging 254
    small print 255
    substandard work 254
    your rights 11–12
servicing
    gas boilers 33, 34
    patio heaters and gas barbecues
        84
shantung 164
sheepskin 164
shelves, kitchen units 60
shirt-fronts, rucking 171
shock, first aid 263–4
shocks, electric 261
shoe polish stains 206, 213
shoes
    canvas 155
    cleaning 161, 165
    stain removal 205, 207
    trainers 184
shopping 10–18
    electrical appliances 15–16
    extended warranties 15–18
    from home 12–13
    internet shopping 13
    your rights 11–12
    see also individual goods and
        services
shower curtains, removing
    mildew 201
showers
    choosing 27–8
    cleaning 112–13
silicone sprays, ironing 87
silk 165
    mending tears 219
silk vinyl emulsion paint 68
silver, cleaning 129–30
silver plate, cleaning 130–1
silverfish 243
Silverstone pans 95
sinks
    blockages 217, 220
    choosing 62–3
    cleaning 131–2
    cracked sealant 217
    taps 63–4
sisal floor covering 50
    cleaning 121
skin
    burns and scalds 259
    rashes 263
    removing super glues 188
    sunburn and windburn 264
    see also wounds
slate floors 51
    cleaning 121
slatted bed bases 29

Small Claims Court 249, 254
small print, contracts 255
smells
    fabric deodorisers 180
    lingering smells on hands 233
smoke alarms 104
sofabeds 30–2
sofas, disposal of 230
soft furnishings, care and cleaning
    172–81
soft sheen emulsion paint 68
soft toys 182
soleplates, steam irons 88
solid emulsion paint 68
solid fuel, central heating 34
solid-top bed bases 29
soot, stain removal 206
sorbets, ice cream machines 87
soy sauce, stain removal 206
spa baths, cleaning 112
speakers
    stereo systems 100, 101
    televisions 102
specks, in paintwork 226
spits, gas barbecues 81
splinters, first aid 264
sports bags 182
spring interior mattresses
    care of 175
    choosing 29–30
sprung-edge bed bases 29
squeaking doors 219
squeaking floorboards 220
squirrels 244
stain removal 186–213
    see also individual types of stain
stain-resistant treatments
    carpets 48
    curtains 57
stainless steel
    cutlery 140–1
    garden furniture 85
    irons 88
    knives 92
    pans 95, 149–50
    sinks 63, 132
    work surfaces 62, 135
Stanley 36
static electricity 156
steam cleaners 104
steam generator irons 88
steam irons 87–8
steamer chairs 84
steel
    baths 27
    garden furniture 85
    see also stainless steel
stereo systems 100–1
stick blenders 77